A GROUNDING FOR LIFE

A History of
Maltman's Green School

that 'tackle anything' quality

To Miriam with love

Cynthia

Cynthia Walton
with Pauline E. Hodder

Barn*books*

DEDICATION
To my parents, Tree
and Harry Morris,
for their imagination,
courage and good
sense, in giving me
a life-enhancing
experience at
Maltman's Green.

All orders and enquiries to:

BARN BOOKS Ltd
2 Beaumont Grove
Solihull
West Midlands B91 1RP

Published by
BARN BOOKS Ltd.
Copyright © 2004

ISBN 0-9540519-2-0

Printed by
Orphans Press Ltd.
Leominster

*Cover illustration and logo
by Pauline E. Hodder*

CONTENTS

MALTMANS GREEN

While it is quite possible to state clearly the aims of a school like Maltman's Green, it is not so easy to be explicit about the methods by which those aims are achieved. In fact "method" is too rigid a word to use in connection with the bringing up of children, where all must be flexible and capable of change – where, indeed, the only fixed principle is the keeping of an open mind. If one way proves to be a blind alley, there is nothing for it but to try another way… To make up one's mind finally about a child is like putting a kitten in splints. This capacity for change is really a sensitiveness and an adaptability to the child's point of view.

Beatrice Chambers, MA Dublin

FOREWORD

It is a pleasure to contribute a Foreword to this book. Mrs Walton asked me to do so, having read that I was arguing for children's control over their own learning at school (Mayall, 2003). Of course, that is an old argument, but it is still necessary today, especially in the light of current education policy for the state system.

The ideas put into practice by Miss Beatrice Chambers form part of a long tradition in European thought, dating back at least to Froebel and Montessori. In England a few schools, at any one time, have acted both as counter-balance and as exemplars in relation to mainstream education thinking and practice. In the 1930s, Hadow (1931) was enunciating the value of 'providing fields of new and interesting experiences to be explored', by appealing 'less to passive obedience and more to the sympathy, social spirit and imagination of the children', with less 'mass instruction and more individual and group work'. But it took time, and the intervention of a world war, before these principles, again enunciated – in the Plowden Report (1967), gained wide acceptance, and before some of them, in some places, were put into practice.

This book provides a valuable case-study of one of the pioneering schools of the 1930s. In drawing on the memories of those who spent time there, as well as on documents and photos, it leads us into understanding of how such a school was experienced. Even today, it is still unusual to put children's knowledge and experience centre stage when describing a school.

As well as providing an interesting and delightful record, the book stands as part of the history of educational experiment – a valuable resource for people working for better experiences for our children.
I wish it every success.

Berry Mayall, Professor of Childhood Studies

Institute of Education, University of London

INTRODUCTION

Anyone who ever went to Maltman's Green School (MG), in the era of its founder, Miss Beatrice Chambers, had an unforgettable experience. I was at MG for four years from 1937 to 1941 and my philosophy of life, my love of music and the arts, stems from that time. I kept up with only one MG friend throughout the ensuing years, but often thought of other girls and how I would like to meet them again. Unfortunately, I did not know about the MG reunions in 1983 in London and Knaresborough.

In the autumn of 2001, I was leafing through *Saga Magazine*, when I came across an advertisement from pupils of different schools, suggesting a reunion. So I decided to do the same and inserted an advertisement saying 'How about a reunion or writing a book about MG?'

I received seven replies from this advertisement, which led me on to 15 people at the outset. Unbeknown to me, Pauline Hodder, who had been Head of Art at MG from 1968 to 1990, had been building up a substantial archive about the school. This included *The History of the Building and the Grounds*, correspondence with various people who had been at MG in Miss Chambers' era, and various letters, memories and other information about the Headmistresses and the school from Miss Burke's to Mrs Evans' time.

I met Pauline Hodder and she kindly lent me copies of her archives, including an account of MG specially written by Ruth Behrens. Miss Julia Reynolds, the present Headmistress, sent me a mass of interesting material and provided photographs of MG's Headmistresses, new school buildings and current activities.

The main section of the book is about Miss Chambers' era, from 1918 to 1945 – from the time when the school was founded until she died. This was the period when her philosophy of education was put into practice at MG.

Ruth Behrens, who was at MG from 1934 to 1941, has written a very lively history of her experience, packed with invaluable information about every aspect of the school. She has kindly allowed me to incorporate some of this material into this book, without always giving her due credit. Her sister, Mary Behrens, has also contributed vital pieces of information.

Another source of information was the booklet about the MG Reunion in 1983, compiled by Caty Early and Mary Behrens. This had quotes about MG and Miss Chambers from letters received by Mary Behrens; a list of names (and married names) and addresses of all the old girls who attended; gleanings from other letters and conversations about the lives of numerous old girls; and *In Memoriam*. I have quoted from this booklet without asking permission, and apologise in advance for doing so.

In 2002, I wrote to the MG contacts who had replied to me and they have all been very forthcoming with information about their period at the school. I must particularly thank Peggy Neal Green, who was at the school both as a pupil and as assistant Matron, in 1939, and who had a very close relationship with Miss Chambers. I was able to meet her and she has been a fount of knowledge.

One of the copy letters in the archive was from Mrs Caroline Wakely in 1983. On the off-chance she would still be at the same address 20 years later, I wrote to her and received a mass of information about her mother's family. Her mother was one of five sisters who went to MG and there were also a further four cousins. I contacted members of this family who sent me their personal accounts of MG. I was able to visit Helen Robinson, one of the sisters, whom I taped. She was an old girl and also returned to teach at MG. She also lent me a book of photographs and MG Christmas cards which I have been able to copy. Other interesting photos and illustrations have come from Ruth Behrens, Peggy Neal Green, Christine Hutchinson and Shirley Massey. Caroline Wakely sent me a collection of her mother's school reports with lino cut headings which were used by the whole school between 1925 and 1935.

The chapter on the history of the building has been based on the work of Jennie Fletcher, a former bursar at the school. She has carried out the research into the history of the building from the Head Office of the Society of Friends in London, Jordans Friends Meeting House and the Parish Church of Chalfont St. Peter. The description of the house when the Drummond family lived there comes from *Memories of Maltman's Green* recollected and written by Algernon Drummond, one of the sons of the owner. I must thank the Editor of *The New Statesman* for permission to reproduce a page of advertisements for schools in 1937. I would like to thank Caroline Wakely for permission to reproduce a school report of Marion Robinson.

I would like to thank the following people who have shared their knowledge of MG with me, or whom I have quoted: Mary Behrens, Ruth Behrens (Boo), Enid Berridge, Paula Burke, Miss Charters, Joyce Cutbush, Hazel Dodds, Caty Early, Eleanor Early (Oll), Patsy Fowler, Nora Kay, Christine Hutchinson, Bubbles Lemon, Audrey Lovibond, Bridget Luard, Barbara McMurray, Dorothea McMurray (Dorrie), Rosemary Naylor, Pamela Neal Green, Peggy Neal Green, Jane Noel, Alison Nugent, Mary Riley, Helen

Robinson, Diana Sanderson (Dinkles), Susan Sanderson, Olive Scott, Caroline Wakely.

The history of MG since 1945 consists of memories of staff rather than former pupils. It has come mainly from Pauline Hodder's archive material. The written memories of a remarkable quartet of teachers, each with more than 20 years teaching at MG, from Pauline Hodder, Head of Art, Pat Journet, Head of Physical Education, Shirley Massey, Head of Music, and Wendy Wilson, Head of Science have been invaluable. Madeleine Evans, Headmistress from 1988 to 1998, has sent me her printed yearly addresses to the Friends of Maltman's Green, and both she and Julia Reynolds have sent me written material about their aims and ethos.

I have also had access to many of the old MG magazines and have used material and illustrations from them without asking permission and apologise in advance for doing so. I can not trace Camelot Press, publishers of *The Modern Schools Handbook*, and have therefore quoted from it without permission.

Maltman's Green was a unique school and, although it has changed over the years, it still appears to hold dear some of the philosophy which inspired Miss Chambers to found the school. It has also continued to this day its wonderful tradition of music-making, started under Miss Ruby Holland in 1918 – with the school winning the BBC Junior *Songs of Praise* School Choir of the Year in 2003.

I have tried to include the names and the personal experiences of many old girls. If I have misquoted or made glaring omissions, I apologise and you must put it down to a 'senior moment'. It has been great fun getting in touch with so many old girls and, judging by the letters I have received, we have all enjoyed a long, nostalgic wallow.

I would like to thank Professor Berry Mayall for her kind Foreword and good wishes. Finally I must thank my husband Kenneth and my daughters Ruth and Su for their patience in reading my MSS and for their helpful suggestions. They have been invariably encouraging and have corrected my spelling mistakes and punctuation. Ruth has also edited my material. I would also like to thank the book's designer, Ted Kinsey, for his expertise.

CYNTHIA WALTON, December 2003

HEADMISTRESSES AND MILESTONES

Miss Beatrice Chambers, Girton College, Cambridge, MA Dublin.
Head: 1918–1945

Maltman's Green was founded in 1918 by Beatrice Chambers, as a progressive girls' boarding school, to provide a unique educational experience for girls from the age of 8 to 18. Previously the Head of Huddersfield High School, Miss Chambers obtained the backing of parents and friends, to put her new educational ideas into practice. It was a school with no rules, no marks, no exams and voluntary attendance at lessons. Its aim was to develop character and intellect, to encourage self-expression, and to increase resource and initiative through practical work. As well as normal academic subjects, girls went to carpentry and pottery classes. There was great emphasis on the arts, especially music, which has run like a golden thread in the school for over 75 years.

'To enable children to be themselves – that is, to put them in full possession of their lives – is the aim of Maltman's Green. The children must gain by experience the wisdom which will enable them to live those lives so that the world itself may be enriched by them.'

Miss Theodora Lowe, BA Oxon.
Head: 1945–1957

Miss Lowe had previously taught at Harrogate College, which had a formal attitude to education. She herself taught English and encouraged those who produced good work, but was critical of girls who failed to reach her high standards. She took an interest in every girl, but her prime concern was exam success. Certain freedoms were curtailed – attendance at lessons became compulsory and girls in Group VI could no longer wear home clothes, but had to continue wearing school uniform. However, the arts continued to flourish, and the old school pottery which had fallen into disuse was revived in the 1950s. Old girls at MG have vivid memories of 'Theo sailing into prayers each morning, her black gown flowing behind her and a pile of books under her arm'.

Miss Paula Burke, NSS. Teaching Diploma of the National Froebel Foundation.
Head: 1958–1978

Soon after Miss Burke was appointed, a radical decision was made to change the school into a preparatory boarding and day school for girls from the age of 5 to13, and to prepare girls for the Common Entrance exam. Four years later, there was a crisis when the Royal Bank of Scotland, which held the freehold, wished to take over the lease of the house and grounds for a housing development. After strong opposition, there was victory for parents, pupils and local residents. The school then developed its curriculum and buildings to accommodate new maths and more science teaching. A new well-equipped science laboratory was built and a new outdoor swimming pool constructed. New Heads of Science, Art, Music and PE were appointed, who had the freedom to develop their subjects creatively.

'What the brain does not remember the hands do' was Miss Burke's Credo.

Mrs Barbara Asprey, Certificate of Education, Cambridge.
Head: 1977–1988

This was a period of great expansion in school numbers and buildings. The school acquired the freehold of the grounds and the buildings, a prerequisite for Maltman's Green acquiring charitable status. Then new building plans went ahead. First the old coachhouse (art room) and greenhouse (pottery) were demolished and a new block built with classrooms and an art room. Next came a Music block and then a Gym block, the *Lapraik Hall*. Another new Science block was built to house senior and junior laboratories and a computer room. The arts, especially music, continued to flourish and an orchestra was founded. Gymnastics became very popular, with the school team among the championship winners in many of the countrywide Under-10, Under-11 and Under-13 competitions.

Mrs Madeleine Evans BA (Hons), PGCE.
Head: 1988–1998

The school continued to excel in the academic field, as well as in the arts and physical education. The old house was seen as the heart of the school; every year, there were new buildings, blending in with the old house and linked to it by cloister-like covered ways. These included a science wing with information and design technology centres, a classroom block with a language laboratory, a kindergarten wing and a new assembly hall. In 1995 a momentous decision was made to cease boarding.

'My aim is for every child to discover a talent while she is at MG. Will your child discover a talent for a particular subject not necessarily an academic one? Did you know that she had perfect pitch, a flair for design, the suppleness and control to do a backward somersault? Has she discovered a talent for friendship? A talent for compromise? A talent for leadership? A talent for working as part of a team? I cannot over-stress the importance for the future of co-operative work skills.'

Miss Julia Reynolds BEd (Hons).
Head: 1998 to the present day

Today, Maltman's Green is a large, thriving non-denominational preparatory day school for girls from the age of 3 to 11. Academically flying high, the school also excels in arts and sport. Each pupil has a PE lesson every day as Miss Reynolds believes that good physical health and the highest level of intellectual attainment are inextricably linked. An indoor swimming pool complex is currently being built. The school followed its strong musical tradition by winning the Junior Schools *Songs of Praise* Choir of the Year in 2003.

'Girls are encouraged to aim high and face life's challenges philosophically and with enthusiasm. To give of one's best and not to crumple at the first hurdle, is paramount. As with sport, team effort is crucial, whether in the choir, the orchestra or in the classroom and learning to work together and to share is one of the most valuable lessons in life. As well as achieving high educational standards, Maltman's Green aims to foster personal qualities such as self reliance, determination, confidence and respect for others.'

CHAPTER ONE

THE HISTORY
OF THE
BUILDING
AND GROUNDS

THE QUAKER ASSOCIATION

'Sufferings' by Besse records that William Grimsdale of Maltman's Green had cows to the value of £7 18s taken from him in 1676 and, in 1684, he forfeited goods to the value of £2 12s.

The 1700s

Maltman's Green past is connected with the Quakers, who had their Meeting House at Jordans in Chalfont St. Peter. William Grimsdale, who lived with his wife, Alice, in the house in 1675, was a yeoman farmer with 20 acres of land. They were Quakers, who attended Sunday meetings at Jordans, a couple of miles away.

In those days, Quakers were persecuted for their faith and some used to meet at *Hungry Hill*, a house in Coleshill, in Hertfordshire. As they were on the edge of the county, this group was largely ignored, whilst Quakers in Buckinghamshire were persecuted. Each Quaker group kept a book of *Sufferings*, in which they recorded the imprisonments, fines and problems they faced. *Sufferings* by Besse records that William Grimsdale of Maltman's Green had cows to the value of £7 18s taken from him in 1676 and, in 1684, he forfeited goods to the value of £2 12s.

William was a respected elder, called a *Weighty Quaker* by the Society of Friends, and would have known William Penn, Isaac Pennington and Thomas Ellwood, the leading Quakers in the local community. He was one of the original trustees of the land at Jordans, where the meeting house was built – the land having been purchased in 1684 by John, son of Isaac Pennington, and put in trust for the Quakers. As a *Public Friend*, William Grimsdale might preach the gospel and give public testimony to his faith. He also officially signed many documents and was authorised to carry funds to High Wycombe and Amersham for the relief of the poor.

The 1800s

In his will of 1712, Thomas Ellwood left £10 to William Grimsdale, Maultster, 'to be distributed for the help, relief and benefit of much of my poor ffriends called Quakers as he shall judge most fitt to receive same'. This is the only evidence that Grimsdale was a maltster and, perhaps, this is the origin of the name *Maltman's Green*.

William Grimsdale died in 1716, but his widow continued to live at Maltman's Green until 1718. In Chalfont St. Peter's church, there is a copy of an old rate, made in 1718, to collect money for rebuilding the church tower, which had collapsed in 1708. Included in the entry is shown: 'Widow Grimsdale, Maltman's Green, Quaker – £6'.

Both Grimsdales and their son, John, are buried in the green in front of Jordans Meeting House, where the Penn gravestones can also be seen. A list of burials and a plan of the burial site are still kept at the Meeting House.

From 1720 onwards, Maltman's Green was occupied by a succession of small farmers and others – Proby Saunders, Robert Stevens, Mr Gregory, William Greenaway and Widow Hunt. In 1803 *Maltman's Green Farm*, comprising Maltman's Green House, two barns, a carthouse and 19 acres of land, was sold to Thos. Ludby of Orchard Farm, Gerrards Cross. In 1818 Thomas Peake was granted a piece of wasteland, from the corner of a field adjoining the

Maltman's Green 1823

Command the Roofe, great Genius, and from thence
Into this house, poure downe thy influence.
That through each room a golden pipe may run
Of living water by thy Benizon.
Fulfill the Larders, and with strengthening bread
Be ever more these Bynns replenished.
Next, like a Bishop consecrate the ground,
That luckie Fairies here may dance their Round;
Charme then the chambers, make the beds for ease
More than for peevish pining sicknusses.
Fix the foundation fast, and let the Roofe
Grow old with time, but yet keep weatherproof.

17th Century Blessing.

ancient freehold lands, and premises of Maltman's Green House. Tenants named Peake were shown paying rent until 1853. In 1847 the name of the house was changed – first to *Milton Green* and then to *Milton Hill*. In 1855 J.M Teesdale, steward of the manor of Chalfont St.Peter, paid rent, and, in 1858, the land was granted to him, until it was transferred to A. H. Drummond in 1884. When Drummond bought the house, it had four bedrooms and 13 acres of land. He bought a further 9 acres of grounds and changed the name of the house back to *Maltman's Green*.

THE DRUMMOND RESIDENCE

Algernon Heneage Drummond had served in the Rifle Brigade in India and retired as a Captain in 1879. He then married Margaret, Elizabeth Benson and, shortly after, began work assisting in the management of Drummonds Bank, working there for 25 years. Both husband and wife came from artistic families. Captain Drummond was a keen artist and had a good tenor voice. He composed the music of the *Eton Boating Song*. Mrs Drummond worked fine embroidery and tapestry. One of her brothers was Sir Frank Benson, the Shakespearean actor, while another was W.A.S. Benson, a pupil and friend of William Morris. Her portrait was painted by Sir William Richmond, RA and exhibited at the Royal Academy. She was one of Sir Edward Burne-Jones' models and was the model for his picture *King Cophetua and the Beggar Maid,* painted in 1884, now at Tate Britain, in London.

A deeply Christian couple, the Drummonds had seven sons and two daughters. The house had to be enlarged as the size of the family increased. W.A.S. Benson designed the additional rooms, many with pendant *Art Nouveau* light fittings, which are still in the building. Their son, Algernon, described the building in minute detail.

'The front door opened into a small entrance hall, containing an oak chest for travelling rugs, a stick and umbrella stand, a very large brass kettle containing maize for pigeons, a wall map of the district, and a few hooks for riding crops, etc. Beyond the entrance hall and behind a curtain, was a large inner hall, which was tiled and extended in height to well above the ceiling of the first-floor rooms. It was spanned by two or three large beams. The staircase led up to a gallery on two sides. The paint was an attractive lightish blue, with red pillars. Above the staircase was a series of windows with family coats-of-arms in stained glass. Downstairs was a beautiful drawing room with a small conservatory leading out of it, and a large bow window at the far end. The sections of this window were in attractive, artistic, oval metal frames.

There was a small room just inside the front entrance, known as the library. Off the inner hall, came a room called *Venice*, named after the architect's wife. At the top of one wall, a semi-circular arch opened onto a staircase leading up to the nursery and the spare room suite. The dining room, panelled in cedar, had a low window at one end and a narrow conservatory at the other. Beyond the foot of the nursery stairs was a brick passage, leading to the garden and conservatory.

The drawing room in 1911

'On the first floor, over the drawing room, was my mother's bedroom, with a similar bow window. It had a fine four-poster bed, round the top of which my mother had embroidered the hangings with the arms of various ancestors. There were two large spare rooms. On the second floor, a steep step led up to a balcony. This was about seven feet wide and on this, in warm weather, the family slept in rows under the stars, on mattresses which were easily rolled up and carried inside if it rained. On the balcony was a flag-pole, usually flying the family flag (three wavy bars quartered with the red lion of Scotland, on a yellow background) or, sometimes, the royal flag of Scotland. On the outside of the building, set into the wall underneath an upstairs window, is the Drummond coat-of-arms. From another position on the balcony one could look down on to what was known as *the Street*. This was a long, narrow, paved courtyard on to which windows opened from all sides – the stained glass windows of the hall looking like a church. Several of the rooms on the first floor were on different levels, with the result that there were no less than ten short sets of stairs. One of these led to the 'pulpit'; this was an extension of the gallery round the corner with a curved recess overlooking the hall and diagonally opposite the head of the front-stairs. One of the family discovered that there was a small window near the front door which did not belong to any room, and eventually an entrance was secretly constructed into a chamber which was about ten feet long, four feet wide and only about three feet high. Two steps were cut out of the stairs and strengthened so that they could easily be removed and did not creak when stepped upon.

'Between the chimneys, outside above the dining room, hung a large bell for use in case of fire, and as a warning bell at a quarter of an hour before lunch. Between the stables and dining room were two large rooms. The first one was used as a studio and later as a workshop and the second, which was raised up about three feet, housed some carriages, but there were holding doors between the two rooms so that it could be used as a stage.

'The house was lit by oil lamps and candles. The lamps for the best rooms were made of copper with brass fittings and had large pink silk shades. They were designed by Mrs Drummond's brother, W.A.S. Benson, for his shop in Bond Street which was run in conjunction with William Morris. Candles were put out in the hall for carrying to the bedrooms, some having glass shades to keep off the draught.

'The house faced south, with a short drive circling a small round lawn with a sundial in the centre. To the east were two small lawns and then three brick steps down to a large lower lawn, with an apple tree and two yew trees. Further east there was a large oak tree surrounded by an iron seat.

'To the south-west of the house were the stables, with at least two single stalls and two loose-boxes, a coach house, a potting shed, a forge and two greenhouses. To the west, a long pergola led to the tennis lawn, beyond which was a field, and then a farm with two semi-detached cottages for the coachman and gardener. To the north-west, there was a large walled kitchen garden. Apart from vegetables, this had apple trees, strawberries, raspberries, gooseberries, pears, plums, peaches, apricots, nectarines and greengages. At the north-east corner of the kitchen garden was a wind-mill, on top of a three-storied, white tower which pumped water to the house. The floors were used for storing fruit and vegetables. At the north-west corner was Mr Drummond's summer house, *The Chalet*. Beside this outside wall was a woodshed. Further north was a plantation known as *the Forest*. Through this, there was a path leading to two connected ponds, one of these was used by the cows, and railed off, the other surrounded by a clay bank planted with shrubs.'

Staffing

At the turn of the century, the Drummonds employed numerous servants to care for their large house and family. A cook, kitchen maid, and scullery maid provided meals. A butler, footman, housemaid, and under-housemaid attended to the running of the household and cleaning. Mrs Drummond employed a ladies' maid, and a nurse, nursemaid, and a governess took care of the children. On special occasions, the staff were supplemented by some of the chief messengers from the Bank. These were in evidence for example, for the 21st birthday of the eldest son, when a dance took place in the dining room, with a Hungarian orchestra specially hired for the night.

Frequent visitors to the house were the three Bowes-Lyons girls, first cousins of Queen Elizabeth, the Queen Mother. Their mother was A. H. Drummond's first cousin, who married the younger son of Lord Strathmore.

Domestic animals

The Drummonds kept a veritable menagerie of animals – some to provide food for the larder and others for the edification and amusement of the children. There were bantams, guinea fowl, a turkey, and several chickens, which supplied the family with eggs and roast fowl. There were also a goat and two pig-sties for a family of pigs which could use up the household waste. Presumably a local butcher slaughtered and cured sides of pork. There is no mention of cows, so the Drummonds must have obtained milk from a neighbouring farm, as well as using their goat for this purpose. As pets and ornamentation, there were two peacocks, a number of white fantail pigeons, a dove, parrot and bullfinch and a dog and a cat.

CHAPTER TWO

MISS
CHAMBERS'
ERA
1918–1945

The favourite carol of girls in the 1930s

MALTMAN'S GREEN BECOMES A SCHOOL

Standing in lonely splendour among the vegetable gardens was the Lone Pine which featured on many of the school lino-cut designs and posters.

Maltman's Green was founded in Gerrards Cross, Buckinghamshire as a progressive girls' boarding school in 1918 by Beatrice E. Chambers (MA Dublin), to provide a unique educational experience to girls from the age of 8 to 18. The school survived 25 years under her guidance until 1943, when she retired due to ill-health. It continued, with various hiccups, for a further 15 years, until 1958, when it became a girls' preparatory school. Today, it is a well-established girls' preparatory day school for girls from the age of 3 to 11. It became a Charitable Trust in 1967, under a Board of Governors, and the Headmistress is a member of the Independent Association of Preparatory Schools.

When Huddersfield Municipal High School (now Greenhead High School) opened in 1908, Miss Chambers was appointed as its Headmistress. Although the school was successful and held in high regard, she was not satisfied with the education it provided. Nor, under the limitations imposed both by the numbers in the school and government by a local authority, did she feel it possible to give her girls the full freedom and opportunities which she considered essential.

With no financial reserves, but with the courage of her convictions, she obtained the backing of parents and friends in Huddersfield, among them Sir Michael Sadler, which enabled her to buy Maltman's Green for £4,000 and set up the school.

When Miss Chambers was looking for a building for her new school, it must have been through her friendship with Miss Ruby Holland that she first heard about Maltman's Green, and later decided to buy the property. Miss Holland, who was Miss Chambers' colleague, friend and closest companion throughout her time at the school, had an earlier connection with Maltman's Green. 'One of my elder sisters founded the first school for English girls in Buenos Aires around 1900. Some pupils there, named Guy, were cousins of the Drummonds and, from 1911, Mr Drummond lent or rented Maltman's Green to another large family of Guys.' Through this connection abroad, Miss Holland was contacted by the Guy family in England, and asked to provide their children with a musical education. She sent a young music teacher to the Guys once a week and she visited herself, once a term, to examine and advise.

When Miss Chambers bought Maltman's Green from the Drummonds in 1918, she and Miss Holland must have been quite convinced of the suitability and possibilities of the building and the extensive grounds for use as her school.

The large, white-panelled entrance hall

The entrance door led into a large, galleried, white-panelled hall, with the main staircase going up to the first floor. In the middle of the hall was a large, round, dark oak table and a grandfather clock stood against the far wall. The Drummonds had placed water pipes in various places; one set was beneath a long wooden seat in the hall beside the stairs, just across from Miss Chambers' drawing room. This was appositely known as *Hot Seat*, well remembered by girls in the 1930s and 1940s, where girls sat and waited if Miss Chambers wished to see them. Opposite the front door there was a small office for the school secretary. There was supposed to be a secret room where a Cavalier had hidden during the Civil War – the small window to the right of the entrance porch had three panes on the outside, but only two inside. This was supposed to indicate a hiding place under the small flight of stairs on the landing above.

To the right of the hall was the drawing room, the Headmistress's sanctum. This was a beautiful room, panelled in white, with an ebony baby grand piano and comfortable sofas. Above the fireplace, there was a white mantlepiece with a concave, recessed shelf, with a ribbed shell effect.

The drawing room – the Headmistress's sanctum

The shelf held an assortment of ornaments of little animals of every description – dogs, turtles, chickens, horses, made of wood or china. French windows at the back of the room led to the conservatory, beyond which were lawned gardens with a wonderfully large magnolia tree.

The archway in the hall led to a library, a small tutorial room and a large room, which was used as the Senior Common Room. From the library, on the right-hand side, there was a second staircase to the first floor and a small staircase to the dining room. Then came a cloakroom with a red, tiled floor, which led into the games cloakroom, where the lacrosse sticks were kept, and *Brick Passage*. On the left was *Stable Yard*, which formed a wing on the left-hand side of the entrance drive, where the old stables had been turned into group rooms, in which the girls had their lessons. The largest room had a stable door to the yard beyond. The smaller adjoining group room had a corn-measure shute from a small loft-like study room above. Beyond *Stable Yard* was the art room (the old coach house), another class room and the pottery, converted from the Drummond's greenhouse.

Stable Yard

Throughout the 1920s and 1930s, additional buildings were built to accommodate extra activities and the expansion of staff. Additions on the ground floor included a hall, used as a gym, a theatre, for dancing classes, and where the school gathered for a Sunday evening meeting; a dining room, a carpenter's shop, a laboratory, a Matron's room, three extra music rooms and three group rooms. Further sleeping accommodation was later provided by *Retreat*, with space for 15 girls on the ground floor in separate cubicles, or small rooms.

All the other dormitories were on the first and second floors of the house. When Dinkles Sanderson went to MG in 1926, her dormitory for several terms was *Zoo*, above the drawing room. Other dormitories were *Big Room*, overlooking the front of the house, and above it *Balcony*, *Haven* and *Day Nursery*. Along the corridor were *Serbian Stripes*, with an upright piano for practising, and *Rose Cretonne*, near to the airing cupboards. Looking out to the back garden next to *Pond Meadow*, (a large music room) were *Pond 1* and *Pond 2*, specially designed dormitories with built-in individual cupboards against one long wall.

Baths

There were two communal bathrooms, one near *Big Room* with four baths and the other at the far end of the house with three baths. There was no privacy, but girls of the same age bathed together. Some girls were allowed the use of a single bathroom, as long as there were no visitors.

The dining room was light and airy

The dining room

The dining room was a purpose-built, flat-roofed, wooden building, not unlike a very large cricket pavilion. It was light and airy and hung with pictures by mainly modern artists, such as John Nash and Christopher Wood, supplied by The School Prints firm. Pictures were changed each term. Against the far wall stood a large oak dresser with a display of gleaming copper coffee pots and Brittany pottery.

The grounds

The grounds were a delight. A large chestnut tree stood at the entrance gate and the wisteria-clad frontage was beautiful. A series of lawns, surrounded by large fir trees, stretched down to a minor playing field, the main (lacrosse) field being across the road directly opposite the school. Beyond these again were vegetable gardens and orchards. Standing in lonely splendour among the vegetable gardens was the *Lone Pine*, which featured on many of the school lino-cut designs and posters. In 1968, a new gym block, with group rooms above it, was built right next to the *Lone Pine*, which then stood at one corner of the block. In 1990, when there were severe gales and hurricanes, the tree branches bent over and touched the classroom windows. Concerned parents insisted the tree should be felled.

The Lone Pine

Staff housing

While some of the staff slept in the school building, others slept in converted cottages just down the road from MG. Miss Chambers sometimes slept in her flat at the school, but in the 1930s bought *The Bolt*, a nearby house, which she shared with Miss Holland.

THE BEGINNING

' "To live indeed," said Sir Thomas Browne, "is to be again ourselves." and, though he was speaking of immortality, his words are true of this present life.'

In the early years of the 20th century, a number of schools were founded by individuals with new ideas about education. These progressive schools included Dartington Hall, A.S. Neill's Summerhill and Dora Russell's Beacon Hill School. In *The Modern Schools' Handbook* (published by The Camelot Press in 1934), Trevor Blewitt, the editor, included chapters by the Heads of eight co-educational schools, five boys' schools and five girls' schools (of which Maltman's Green was one) about their schools and their philosophy.

CO-EDUCATIONAL SCHOOLS TO UNIVERSITY AGE

Beacon Hill School, Bedales School, Dartington Hall School, Frensham Heights School, King Alfred School, St. Christopher's School, Summerhill School

BOYS' SCHOOLS TO UNIVERSITY AGE

Abbotsholme School, Bembridge School, Bryanston School, Dauntsey's School, Leighton Park School

GIRLS' SCHOOLS TO UNIVERSITY AGE

Badminton School, Croham Hurst School, The Farmhouse School, The Garden School, Maltman's Green School

Some ranked as public schools, some were experimental. 'The only features common to them all were, firstly, the rejection of some of the ideas of the conventional Public School system, secondly, the insistence on the needs of the individual child, and lastly, a belief in a changing world.'

Some of the original pupils of Maltman's Green still survive. Their memories of the education they received are as strong as ever, and they look back on their schooldays with affection and pride at having been part of a unique educational experiment.

The fees were high (200 guineas p.a. in 1918 and still the same in 1938, twenty years later!), but the school was never run for profit. Miss Chambers (always known as *Ma* to staff and students, but never addressed to her face as anything other than Miss Chambers) paid the normal salary to herself and to her staff. Any surplus was put aside, both to repay the capital cost incurred in starting the school and, later, to increase the number of staff and erect additional buildings. There was never accommodation for more than 75 girls, as this was the limit Miss Chambers considered necessary to preserve the contact she desired with her 'family'. At the outset, 12 pupils were day girls, but when Miss Chambers decided she only wanted boarders, the day girls left, although one, Enid Berridge, came back to the school again as a boarder.

Miss Chambers outlined her general philosophy and aims for Maltman's Green. ' "To live indeed," said Sir Thomas Browne, "is to be again ourselves." and, though he was speaking of immortality, his words are true of this present life. Life can only be lived in the fullest sense of the word, by those who are truly themselves; and to enable people to be themselves must ultimately be the aim of all psychologists and educationists, though they may approach it by various routes and call it by different names.'

Miss Chambers felt that that the school should not cut off the children from real life, which to most children of school age means family life as opposed to institutional. She wanted the school to provide, as nearly as it could, the circumstances of family life with all that that implies.

Ma believed that, 'according to their age and ability, the children's contributive actions to this joint family life are equal in value and just as essential as those of the adults. To be quite consistent, my school should, of course, be co-educational, but for many reasons – notably my own inability to carry out co-education as I feel it should be carried out, and the unsuitability of the house for the purpose – I knew that I could accomplish what I meant and wanted only if the school were confined to girls. At school, as in the home, the only guide possible where children are concerned is the old nursery one of common sense – common sense borne out by imagination, wise and sympathetic understanding, and an infinite capacity for change.'

She saw this as a sensitiveness and an adaptability to the child's point of view. 'As such, it determines the standard of work. Not that the standard is variable, to be raised or lowered according to each child's capability – far from it. There can be but one criterion for any piece of work whether in school or in the world – the criterion of reality. A fixed standard of school excellence may ensure work that is correct and orderly, work that is academically true, but which yet may lack the truth and life without which it is valueless in the world.' To achieve real success in her school, she wanted her staff to be ordinary people in an ordinary world. They had to be masters of technique – to have the power and ability to teach – and they also had to be expert and up to date.

Miss Chambers was acutely aware of the problems of freedom for the child and felt that ideally, children should not be prevented from making mistakes or protected from the consequences of them, so long as someone with greater knowledge and understanding was at hand in case of mishaps.

The flavour of MG could be judged by Ma's unusual attitude to some misdemeanours. Two friends, Olive Scott and Pauline Hambly, slept on the roof outside *Balcony*, and dared each other to climb over the rooftops as far as the bell, which hung between two chimney pots over Ma's flat. Unfortunately, Ma heard noises on the roof over her room and sent Matron to find out about it. When the girls returned to their beds, she was waiting for them, but little was said. A friend of Kato Robinson once dared her to run round the school naked, which she did and encountered Ma, who just looked at her but said nothing, either then or later. Another pair were discovered shopping in the village without permission. Overcome by conscience, they waited on *Hot Seat* to apologise, but Ma refused to listen to them at all, saying, 'No, go away, I do not wish to speak to you.'

As Miss Chambers said, 'Because the children form the crew and not the passengers on board the ship, they develop a sense of responsibility towards other people, and a quiet self-reliance in the conduct of their own lives. Because

The rooftops

of the complete lack of fear in their minds, they have a freedom in their relationships with each other and with the grown-ups in their community that makes for courage and confidence in their daily lives.'

Caty Early, who went to the school in the 1920s, wrote that Miss Chambers treated every situation and everyone as individuals. 'But we had to be responsible individuals, responsible for our actions, for ourselves, for our rights. And we had the freedom to do this. After all, thinking back, the only real rules we had concerned meals and bedtimes. Another thing which helped and which Miss Chambers was most insistent about – we were all mixed up in ages in dormitories, and in the dining room, like a family.' This idea of responsibility was fostered by assigning each new junior girl (a *nipper*) to a senior one (a *nunky*) who helped with the nitty gritty of new boarding school life, the weekly laundry lists, problems with homework, school customs and, initially, with homesickness. 'Miss Chambers had vision and taught us to think for ourselves –

The lawns at the side of the house

it was her genius that made MG such a happy place that we all – staff and girls remember half a century later. We learnt the value of freedom "liberty, not licence," as Miss Chambers used to say.'

The spirit of freedom was such that, for example, none of the girls would ever have dreamed of running up and down the front stairs. If they had, Ma would have emerged from the drawing room with some pithy remark. Somehow, her personality kept the girls in line. Any girl she could not trust would be asked to leave, as the school was unsuitable for her. Lois Hambly only knew of one girl to whom this happened in the five years that she was at MG.

Patsy Fowler had been brought up in an unorthodox fashion, out of doors all day, all year round. When she was 11, she was sent to a boarding school seven miles from her home but, never having

The moon…the beauty of heaven,
The glory of the stars,
An ornament giving light
In the highest places of the Lord.

been confined, she left for home, whenever the doors were open. At 13, she was sent to MG and remembered only two rules – don't climb the trees or get on the roof. When she felt like rushing around the garden in the dark, she would ask permission, which was always granted. Although prep was set, there was no fixed time to do it and she found it much easier to do it than stand up to say she had been too lazy to tackle it.

Miss Chambers wrote, 'All kinds of unexpected developments arise when children are encouraged to be themselves, but they are only temporary, and the girls seem to leave school with a quiet poise and power of discrimination, which is very necessary in the heterogeneous world of today when everyone, if she is to preserve her integrity, must hourly be called upon to choose between the best and the merely mediocre.'

CHOOSING MALTMAN'S GREEN

'The aim of the school is to develop the character, intellect, and healthy growth of the child for the good of the community, to encourage self expression, to increase resource and initiative by practical work.'

Considering Maltman's Green for their daughters' education meant that parents had initially to make two choices. Firstly, did they want to send their child to a modern or a traditional school? Secondly, if a modern school, which one would suit their child best? Parents had to sum up the strengths and weaknesses of their child. Could she concentrate easily? Was she better with her hands than with her head? Had she a particular talent? Was she imaginative? Did she need stimulation or peace and quiet to make the most of her abilities? They also had to look ahead and decide whether the school would be able to provide an education suitable for the girl's future.

What sort of criteria were needed to make a rational choice? Obviously parents had to visit different schools. In their tour of the school, parents had to look at the timetable – how often did their child's best subject occur, what were the leisure activities, what emphasis was given to sport, exercise and rest? How did the girls they met behave? Were they relaxed and friendly and not overly polite? They had to then look at the physical facilities of the school – the classrooms and the provision for art, drama and music. In a boarding school, the dormitories had to be inspected, too, to see if they were pleasant, colourful and comfortable. Was enough attention given to health and were meals appetizing, of good quality and sufficient for the needs of growing girls? The interview with the Head was very important, to discover whether her personality was one to whom parents would safely entrust their child; and to find out about the intellectual level of the school, the qualifications of the staff, and the subsequent careers of old girls.

How far did parents rely on their own resources, and how far were they swayed in their choice by recommendations from friends, old girls, and teachers? Many of the modern schools needed to advertise since they were not all that well-known.

The pupils at MG were drawn from several very specific sources. There were numerous girls from Huddersfield, whose mothers or aunts had been pupils of Miss Chambers at Huddersfield High School or who, like the five Robinson sisters from Tyneside – Elizabeth, Katharine (Kato), the twins, Marian and Helen, and Anne, and Elspeth, their cousin – went to the school each in their turn, because their wise mother wanted that sort of unusual education for her girls. Her husband was a shipowner, who headed a large, prosperous, non-conformist and teetotal family. The Robinsons' cousins – Peggy, Dorrie and Barbara McMurray – also went to MG.

July 3, 1937   THE NEW STATESMAN AND NATION   55

THE charge for classified advertisements is One Shilling and Sixpence per insertion (a line averages seven words). One line should be added for Box Number. Substantial reduction for a series of insertions. Copy first post Wednesday. The Advert. Manager, N.S. & N., 10 Great Turnstile, London, W.C.1. (Hol. 3216.)

LECTURES AND MEETINGS

THE ETHICAL CHURCH, Queen's Road, Bayswater, W.2. Sunday, July 4th, at 11, MR. W. E. COLLIER: "THE ETHICS OF DISCIPLESHIP." 7.0, MR. W. E. COLLIER: "THE CHANGING RELATIONS OF RELIGION AND MORALS."

AEOLIAN HALL, New Bond Street, Theistic Church Service. Sunday, 4th: REV. I. TYSSUL DAVIS, B.A. Subject: "THE LITTLE FURTHER."

THE SEX EDUCATION CENTRE; Unity Theatre Club, Britannia Street, King's Cross. Open Mondays 7-9 p.m. May–July. Library Books 2d. a week; consultations 11. Programme of lectures sent on request.

CONWAY HALL, Red Lion Square, Holborn.— Sunday, July 4th, at 11 a.m.: MORITZ J. BONN, D.SC.: "PROPAGANDA AND INTERVENTION." Admission Free. Visitors welcome.

FREE RELIGIOUS MOVEMENT towards world religion and world brotherhood. Meetings on Sundays at 11 a.m., at Lindsey Hall, The Mall, Notting Hill Gate, W.8. Leader: REV. WILL. HAYES. July 4th: "SANSKRIT FABLES."

LECTURE/SOCIAL, Monday, July 5th at 8 p.m. MR. R. H. WATT: "REALIST FILMS." Youth House Club, 250 Camden Road, N.W.1. Gulliver 5189.

FRUITARIAN COOKERY DEMONSTRATIONS. St. Francis Clinic, 192 Red Lion Square, W.C.1. Tuesdays, July 6th and July 13th at 5 p.m. Questions. Tasting. Write for advice on modern diet.

SUMMER SCHOOL

MARX MEMORIAL LIBRARY AND WORKERS' SCHOOL SUMMER SCHOOLS at GODALMING, SURREY (July 31st to Aug. 28th) and SKEGNESS, LINCS. (July 31st–Aug. 14th). Lecturers include: Emile Burns, Beatrice King, G. R. Strauss, M.P., J. R. Campbell, T. A. Jackson, J. F. Horrabin, William Paul, R. Bridgeman, Victor Gollancz. Fourth week at Godalming (Aug. 21st–28th) reserved for University students, teachers, professional workers. Syllabus includes Symposiums on: "DIALECTICAL MATERIALISM"—Professor H. Levy, Maurice Cornforth. "HISTORY OF SCIENCE"— J. D. Bernal, Dr. Jos. Needham, J. B. S. Haldane. "EDUCATION." Single lectures by J. R. Campbell, Maurice Dobb, MR. F. Pascal, etc. INCLUSIVE CHARGES from £2 per week. Write for Prospectus to THE SECRETARY, Marx House, 37a and 38 Clerkenwell Green, E.C.1.

SCHOOLS AND EDUCATIONAL

CICELY C. WRIGHT, 50 Great Russell Street, London, W.C.1. EXPERT ADVICE given, free of charge, on SCHOOLS: also on trainings for Secretarial, Domestic Science and other professions.

SCHOOLS—continued

BROOKLANDS, Crowborough, Sussex. Pre-prep. school and all-year-round home. Sound early education and racial training. Boys 3-10. Girls 3-12. Trained staff. Exceptional health record. Beautiful surroundings. Apply Headmaster. Crowborough 299.

BEDALES SCHOOL, Petersfield, Hants. (Founded 1893). A co-educational boarding school for boys and girls from 11-19. Separate junior school for those from 5-11. Inspected by the Board of Education. Country estate of 150 acres. Home Farm. Education is on modern lines and aims at securing the fullest individual development in, and through, the community. Headmaster: F. A. MEIER, M.A. (Camb.).

SCHOOLS—continued

ONLY BOOK AUTHORISED BY H.M.C. PUBLIC AND PREPARATORY SCHOOLS' YEAR BOOK. Official Book of Headmasters' Conference and Association of Preparatory Schools. Consult re schools, careers, professions, etc. 10s. 6d. net.—Year Book Press, 31 Museum Street, W.C.1.

SCHOOLS

belonging to the SOCIETY OF FRIENDS (QUAKERS) IN GREAT BRITAIN (with numbers, age-ranges, and non-Friend Fees). BOYS' SECONDARY BOARDING SCHOOLS. Ackworth School, nr. Pontefract 209: 9-18: £110 Bootham School, York ... 145: 12-19: £165 Leighton Park School, Reading ... 150: 12-19: £189 GIRLS' SECONDARY BOARDING SCHOOLS. Ackworth School, nr. Pontefract 172: 9-18: £110 The Mount School, York ... 118: 13-19: £153 CO-EDUCATIONAL SECONDARY BOARDING SCHOOLS. Friends' School, Great Ayton, Yorks 150: 9-17: £81 Friends' School, Saffron Walden, Essex ... ... 202: 10-18: £99 Friends' School, Saffron Walden, Essex (Junior) ... ... 28: 7-10: £99 Sidcot School, Winscombe, Somerset 150: 10-18: £123 Friends' School, Wigton, Cumb. 104: 7-17: £82 11. CO-EDUCATIONAL "MODERN" BOARDING SCHOOL. Friends' School, Sibford, nr. Banbury ... ... 158: 10-17: £81 Apply to School, or to Secretary, Friends Education Council, Friends House, Euston Road, N.W.1.

CHILDREN'S FARM, Romansleigh, N. Devon. For children from 3-12 years. Farm life combined with good education and home care. Trained nurse. Entire charge or short periods—holidays. MRS. VOLKMER, B.A.

WYCHWOOD SCHOOL, Oxford (recognised). Founded 1897. Eighty girls, ages 6-18. Entire charge if desired. Special civics (school House of Commons for weekly debate); literature and art. Small classes, large resident staff. Preparation for universities and professions. Swimming, boating, riding, lacrosse, netball, tennis. Health of school exceptional. Aims: to unite a sound modern education on lines of individual freedom with older standards of courtesy and thought for others. Principals: MARGARET LEE, M.A. (Oxon.); GERALDINE COSTER, B. Litt. (Oxon.). Boarders' Fees 150 guineas.

ST. CHRISTOPHER SCHOOL, LETCHWORTH (recognised by the Board of Education). A thorough education for boys and girls to 19 years, at moderate fees in an open-air atmosphere of ordered freedom and progress. Headmaster: H. LYN HARRIS, M.A., LL.B. (Camb.).

PINEWOOD, CROWBOROUGH, SUSSEX. Home school for boys and girls, 3-12 years, where environment, diet, psychology and teaching methods maintain health and happiness. ELIZABETH STRACHAN. Crowborough 224.

MALTMAN'S GREEN, GERRARD'S CROSS, Head Mistress: MISS CHAMBERS, Girton College, Cambridge, late Head Mistress of the Huddersfield High School. The aim of this school is to develop the character, intellect, and healthy growth of the child for the good of the community, to encourage self-expression, to increase resource and initiative by practical work. The girls will be prepared for the Universities, the Medical Profession, and for advanced work in Music or Art. Fees include Elocution, Dancing, Cookery. Gerrard's Cross is 300ft. above sea-level and is on gravel soil. The house is delightfully situated in its own grounds of 15 acres.

THE FROEBEL PREPARATORY SCHOOL, Colet Gardens, W.14. Nursery class attached. Sound modern education for boys and girls from 2-14 years old.

BEACON HILL SCHOOL. (Founded 1927) Principal: DORA RUSSELL NO CONNECTION WITH ANY OTHER SCHOOL. Has acquired most attractive premises at Kingwell Hall, Timsbury, near BATH, Somerset. 500 feet up, facing the Mendip Hills, large gardens, playing field, swimming bath. Co-educational from two years. From individual freedom through self government to social understanding. Health, happiness, and sound teaching in all subjects combined with practical and creative work. Moderate fees. Apply Dora Russell.

HAWNES SCHOOL, AMPTHILL. Public School on individual lines for girls from 10-19. Playing fields, park, woodland, 93 acres. Riding, swimming. Girls are prepared for the usual examinations, and for University entrance or may specialise in Languages, Art, Music, Domestic Science. Fees £120-£180 p.a.

BRECHIN PLACE SCHOOL for Girls and Boys.— Apply MRS. E. M. SPENCER, 11 Brechin Place, Gloucester Road, S.W.7.

THE COLLEGE, SOUTH LEIGH, OXON, specialises in educational problems of boys from 15 to 19. Coaching for all entrance examinations. 10 years' successes. Careers studied. No abnormal boys.—Apply Director, M. CHANINE-PEARCE, M.A.Oxon, England.

ALPINE COLLEGE. Arveyes-Villars, Switzerland. 4,100 feet. Boys, 12-19. Individual preparation for all English Examinations. Special Modern Languages House for the senior pupils with Swiss master. WINTER SPORTS from December to March. Ideal health conditions. Headmaster: J. M. S. BARNARD, M.A. (Cantab.), who will arrange interviews in London on July 13th and 14th. Particulars from Secretary.

TUITION

RUSSIAN by exper. lady teacher. Refs. Central. Phone. Box 856, N.S., & N., 10 Gt. Turnstile, London, W.C.1.

community. Independent study. Special attention to health and physical development. Pupils prepared for the Universities. Well-qualified staff. Principal, BERTA S. HUMPHREY.

OAKLEA, BUCKHURST HILL, ESSEX (recognised by Board of Education). Girls 8 to 19. P.N.E.U. programmes followed. Individual time-tables for Citizens' over 12. Handicrafts, eurhythmics, gardening, riding in forest, etc. Oxford Examination Centre. Principal: BEATRICE GARDNER.

DR. WILLIAMS' SCHOOL, DOLGELLEY, NORTH WALES. Recognised by Board of Education. Headmistress: MISS E. CONSTANCE NIGHTINGALE, M.A. Endowed School. Moderate inclusive fee for board, tuition and books. Junior Department, ages five to ten.

HALSTEAD PLACE, near SEVENOAKS. Preparatory School, Boys and Girls 7-14. Recognised by the Board of Education. Modern outlook.

receive sound education in usual subjects by modern methods. Nursery Dept. (2-5 yrs.) in delightful playroom with South vita-glass sun-terrace. Vacancies for Sept. in Nursery and for children 5-8 yrs. Apply: LESLIE BREWER, Headmaster. Park 4775.

BURGESS HILL SCHOOL. HAMPSTEAD, LONDON, N.W.2. A Preparatory Day School for boys and girls between the ages of 5 and 13. Headmaster: A. K. C. OTTAWAY, M.A., B.Sc. Art, music, workshop and varied creative activities, besides the usual academic subjects. Entries should now be made for September. Facilities for weekly boarders.

FOR advice on the choice of suitable BOARDING SCHOOLS, TUTORS, or other Educational Establishments for boys or girls of any age, apply to J. & J. PATON, Educational Agents, 143 Cannon Street, London, E.C.4. Tel. Mansion House 5053, stating full details of requirements; or consult PATONS LIST OF SCHOOLS AND TUTORS. 39th Annual Edition. Post free 5s. 6d.

Modern schools' advertisements in *The New Statesman and Nation*, 1937

The school had a reputation for small classes and a good teacher-pupil ratio, with especially good tuition in music, art and drama, that attracted a number of talented girls in those subjects. Several girls had parents with literary or theatrical leanings. These included J. B. Priestley's two daughters, Barbara and Sylvia; Mary Temple Thurston, Jennifer Ramage, the daughter of Cathleen Nesbitt; and Jane Anne Sterndale Bennett, the daughter of the actress, Athene Seyler. Since the school was known for its liberal and left-wing leanings, there were several girls who were daughters of Labour Party intelligentsia, stalwarts and supporters; among them Theresa and Peggy Cripps, daughters of Sir Stafford Cripps; Lois, daughter of Naomi Mitchison; Diana, daughter of Victor Gollancz, the left-wing publisher; and the daughters of Lord Strabolgi and Lord Swaything. Other liberal parents, such as the father of Jo and Hazel Dodds, who had been the Liberal Party Chairman and was editor of a liberal newspaper, and the Scotts of the Manchester Guardian, sent their children to MG and recommended the healthy life and good teacher-pupil ratio to their friends, the liberal and public-spirited parents of Mary and Ruth Behrens in Manchester.

There was also a landed gentry county set, several girls being 'hons', whose future was expected to be the season, presentation at court and marriage. Rosemary Naylor's mother wanted this for her daughter, but Rosemary joined the FANNYS before the war and then the ATS, as a driver in London. Later, she became a plotting officer for the ack ack and served for seven years.

Other parents included enlightened businessmen, such as the Early family, and the parents of Dinkles and Sue Sanderson, whose father was a wine merchant with an interest in natural history and whose mother was a keen supporter of new ideas in education. Peggy Neal Green's father chose the school for his four daughters because the Headmistress was a liberal, he had been dragged round three schools and he was tired! Cynthia Morris' great-aunt had attended Huddersfield High School and her father subscribed to *The New Statesman and Nation*, both these factors predisposed her parents to the school. Jane Noel was sent to MG by her parents but her grandfather said she needed more discipline, so she was taken away and sent to Wycombe Abbey, a more conventional girls' school. How did these girls feel about their parent's choice of Maltman's Green? Did they feel they had benefited from Ma's avant-garde ideas? Did her unusual regime fit them for life in the real world?

Many old girls who went to the MG reunions in 1983 in London and Knaresborough wrote to Mary Behrens, who had organised the event, with positive comments. 'The spirit of MG pervaded the whole venture,' wrote Alison Nugent, 'Ma always loved a job well done – "Finish your work" she used to say, and she would have been proud and greatly appreciative of this occasion. I find that as the years go by, one realises and appreciates more all the time Ma's vision

Old girls – (left to right) Pamela Neal Green, Grizelda Heaton-Armstrong and Joyce Murray

Old girls – (left to right) Sue Sanderson, Ruth Behrens (Boo) and Sylvia Priestley

and ideals and how much she accomplished, and one is so grateful to have been for a time part of her work.' Many girls felt privileged to have been to MG, which helped to mould their actions and characters for the future. Peggy Neal Green had great respect for Ma and her ideas and felt thankful that she turned out girls who had a toughness of mind and body, that helped them cope with the Second World War and a rapidly changing world. Her sister, Pamela, thought that the atmosphere Miss Chambers and her staff had created had been a breeding ground for good citizenship, as well as academic attainment. Her friends at the reunion lunch had a 'tackle anything' quality about them, and whether life had treated them with kindness or adversity, they had looked it in the eye and got on with the job cheerfully. She felt that each one of those people could be depended upon to help in time of need – 'and not to turn round and stare should there be an interruption in a concert!'

Several girls had other views of Ma, not always the happiest. Dorrie McMurray was a redhead and always felt that Ma did not understand or like redheads, so she and Ma never hit it off. Dorrie had not wanted to go to MG at all. She had an enquiring mind and, as she could read and write, she felt she could learn everything she wanted to learn by herself. 'I was a great reader and loved English, history and geography but I knew I would never be interested in anything but basic maths.' Dorrie and her sister, Barbara, were helped to settle into MG by having their cousins, Marian and Helen, as their respective *nunkies*. Barbara had been very ill and needed special attention and was happy at MG. But Dorrie felt that although Ma had wonderful ideas about education, she did not appear to understand young children well or make any allowances for any difficulties they had in their home lives, while Miss Bird and Miss Hirst understood her difficulties. Looking back, Dorrie realised she did get a great deal of benefit from MG, 'but there certainly were other unfortunates like me.'

Ruth Behrens was at the school from the age of 10, and found Ma a rather fearsome personage. 'Many of us were rather frightened of her. She could reduce one to tears with a look, and sometimes I was not even sure what I had done wrong. A member of staff would summon one to see Ma and one would wait outside the drawing room, sitting on *Hot Seat*. My memories of sitting there, waiting interminably for I knew not what, are not of the happiest.' Sue Sanderson also had a constant and enduring memory of *Hot Seat*. 'Waiting to be seen by Ma ranks among the most fearful occasions of my life. She had the uncanny knack of apparently seeing though any physical barrier, including your head, so she always knew what was going on … she had the precise measure of your sins and knew where to pierce your most vulnerable and painful spots.' Luckily Hirsty, the house-mistress, was an unfailing protector and friend. Dinkles Sanderson, who was at the school for over eight years, valued the solace she provided by 'her calm manner, her humour and practical common sense which poured constant oil on troubled waters after visits to Ma in the drawing room.'

Nonetheless, these girls valued their experience at MG. Sue Sanderson thought that Ma's methods were successful in 'instilling a tolerance of other people, their different backgrounds, opinions, unfamiliar tastes and personal foibles that would stand us in good stead in adult life' and would have agreed with the sentiments expressed by Patsy Fowler, who wrote to a friend fifty years later, 'Maltman's Green gave me the most brilliant grounding for life, and the independence and self-control I learnt there have contributed enormously to the unsettled, but fun, life that I have had.' Peggy Neal Green, who contracted polio in 1949 and has been disabled most of her life, has as her philosophy to 'live until I die. It seems to me the only way to enjoy life – you have all the time in the world until it runs out.'

DOMESTIC ARRANGEMENTS

'Edith the cook, who was at MG for years, made the best milk puddings I have ever eaten and magnificent steam puddings, marmalade, chocolate, treacle and spotted dog.'

Arriving at the start of term

Running a boarding school requires considerable organisational skills. Not only must lesson time tables be drawn up, but catering, cleaning and general management of the building and staff are of equal importance if the school is to run smoothly.

Organising the arrival of girls at the beginning of term was the first of MG's domestic arrangements. Some girls arrived at school by car, others travelled by train and arranged to meet a member of staff in the tea room, or on the platform at Marylebone Station in London, by a specific time, for the afternoon train. For girls living outside London, travel to school was quite a business. For instance, the Manchester contingent – the Behrens, Dodds and Scott girls – sent their trunks in advance, and then travelled from Manchester to Euston and from Euston to Marylebone with their hand luggage. Ruth Behrens remembered such luggage as 'not only small suitcases but violins, rabbits in hutches, carpentry creations and so on.' Girls from further north travelled to St. Pancras in a similar fashion. Then the group of girls bound for MG assembled on the Marylebone platform for the half-hour journey to Gerrards Cross.

On arrival at MG, by several taxis from the station, the girls entered the hall, followed by the school *boots* with the hand luggage. The hall was bedlam – trunks everywhere, some closed, some open, with girls scurrying upstairs with their trunk trays to their dormitories. Old hands at the school knew their way around and what was required of them. New girls had to be shown their dormitory and the loo, called the *honkey*, and each was given into the charge of a girl, assigned to them as a *nunkey*, to show them the ropes.

Staffing

When Miss Chambers bought Maltman's Green in 1918, she and a Yorkshire colleague prepared the house as a school themselves, including scrubbing the floor tiles in the hall. She soon employed Emma Shurey as a local domestic help. Her daughter Winnie Shurey worked at the school for 37 years, from 1947 to 1984.

The house was always well cared for, with gleaming white paint everywhere and a bright, Prussian blue carpet with shining brass rods up the stairs from the hall. Up to the start of the Second World War, numerous maids did the housework, cleaned the dormitories, classrooms, bathrooms, kitchens and also served meals in the dining room, wearing white starched aprons and caps. These maids lived on the top floor of the school, reached by a little staircase near *Pond 1*. They all belonged to the Salvation Army and could be seen, dressed in their uniform and navy-trimmed bonnets, going into the village for Sunday service.

However, the pupils had domestic duties too. Once dressed, and before breakfast, they had to strip their beds and turn their mattresses into U-shapes. After breakfast, the beds had to be properly made and, as a finishing touch, each girl had to place her eiderdown on top of the bedspread, in a dimple shape at the end of the bed. Clean sheets were given out once a week.

Clothing

In the 1930s, the school outfitter was Rowe's of Bond Street, a memorable shop with a stuffed horse outside its entrance. The school uniform chosen by Ma was very original, setting MG apart from other schools. For a start, it was purple – a colour chosen, it was said, so as not to clash with redheads! In the winter, juniors (up to the age of 14) wore serge shorts, known as *trucks*, with white aertex blouses, grey wool jumpers, grey boys' ribbed, knee socks with purple stripes, and boys' elastic-sided black leather shoes. On Sundays, girls wore tailor-made serge suits with white blouses and white ribbed, knee socks, or fawn lisle stockings. The suits and coats were stylish enough to be worn in the holidays. Girls in Groups IV and V wore round-necked, fitted serge

The original school uniform included shorts and square-necked tunics

tunics with a flared skirt and black lisle stockings. These were always going into holes and girls used to ink their heels, before eventually mending their stockings. In the early years for outdoors wear there was a dashing purple tweed cloak, much loved by Dinkles Sanderson and her contemporaries, as they could 'swirl it round in a most dramatic fashion'. Later on, outdoor clothes consisted of a purple tweed coat, a navy gaberdine raincoat and black galoshes, which were always worn over indoor shoes. There was a smart blazer with a silvery badge. Summer clothes were the same design, but serge gave way to pale purple cotton. Soft, grey, floppy, boys' cricket hats had to be worn in very sunny weather. Girls in Group VI could wear home clothes all the time except for games.

Apart from uniform, the clothes list itemised pyjamas, a dressing gown, slippers, vests, liberty bodices, navy woollen knickers with separate white cotton knicker linings, lacrosse boots, a travelling rug and an eiderdown. Further items included an enamel mug and a string-net toilet holder, which could only be bought from shops run for the blind. Of course all items had to be name-taped, which took hours of sewing before term began.

After afternoon games, everyone changed into *mufti* for the evening, and had brought a couple of dresses with them to last the term. For many years, velveteen, which was very prone to marks, was stipulated in any colour.

Each week, the girls had to gather together their dirty clothes and put them in individually-named laundry bags to be sent to the laundry. There were also a weekly 'house and mending session', when girls washed their Mason Pearson hairbrushes and learned to darn socks and stockings and sew on buttons. Matron kept a general eye on clothes, and added her own comments to school reports: *… has made a greater effort over her mending this term; … collects a tremendous amount of things around her, her drawers are in a terrible state.*

Meals

Meals were taken in the dining room at rectangular, dark brown oak tables with wooden forms on either side and a chair at each end. Ma had noticed that a little girl with bad table manners, sitting next to other girls of the same age, immediately developed worse table manners. So girls were mixed up in ages at table, as in a family, each headed by a member of staff. In this situation, 'the girl, would soon see her errors and, with no correction other than her own self-respect, she puts the matter right'.

Girls were expected to be punctual for meals, and the dining room door was closed once a meal had begun. Latecomers had to wait on the stairs leading to the dining room, until someone from their table noted their absence and went to the door to invite them in for the meal. Sometimes, there could be quite a long wait, so that the latecomer had to gobble her meal in the remaining time allotted – not good for the digestion!

Outside the Senior Common Room, there was a shelf with a blue curtain where girls had to leave oddments they were carrying with them, labelled, when the bell sounded for meals. e.g. *News Chronicle:* Hazel Dodds. To claim their property, girls had to pay a piece of tuck.

One of the most remarkable things about MG is that girls have vivid memories of really enjoying their food. The food was appetizing and the diet a healthy one. There were three meals a day, with home-made lemonade for elevenses, served in *Brick Passage*. Dorrie McMurray, a pupil in the 1920s, noticed that the food was ordered from Harrods. Dinkles Sanderson thought the food remarkably good for a school. 'Edith the cook, who was at MG for years, made the best milk puddings I have ever eaten and magnificent steam puddings, marmalade, chocolate, treacle and spotted dog.' The whole school took part in the ceremonial stirring of the Christmas pudding at the beginning of the Autumn Term.

Breakfast was cereal, sometimes *pain perdu* – delicious, sizzling, fried slabs of bread, which had been soaked in beaten egg and milk – tea or steaming jugs of creamy coffee, and toast and marmalade. The latter, too, was homemade. Oll Early and Dinkles Sanderson can still savour the smell of marmalade, which pervaded the whole school when the kitchen area was taken over for the making of the year's supply. Some of the girls had fruit breakfasts, their plates filled with dates, apples, oranges, bananas and nuts.

The main meal was at lunch time and supper was at 6pm. Supper was a light meal and might consist of a large baked potato with melting cheese inside it, known as *cheese dreams*. There was plenty of fresh vegetables and fruit. Apples and whiteharte cherries grew in abundance in the gardens and, in season, girls were given handfuls of cherries after meals, but woe betide the girls who left cherry stones around.

There was no 4 o'clock tea, although the few girls who tended to lose weight during term were given a small plate of thin brown bread and honey sandwiches in Matron's room. At the beginning of term, girls brought back tuck (sweets and chocolates), but they were not allowed to keep it for themselves; it had to go into a general pool in the tuck cupboard. Trustworthy girls in the top groups were appointed to sort out and distribute the tuck after lunch – four pieces for each girl on two weekday afternoons, and six pieces on Sundays. A great deal of swapping and trading went on in the library afterwards. Behind the farm, a path led through the woods and fields out on to the main road opposite a shop called Ezra's, where some girls remember escaping to buy illicit sweets. On summer Saturday afternoons the Walls' ice-cream man on his 'Stop me and buy one' tricycle came to the road outside the farm. There was always a queue of girls ready to spend their 4d on various combinations of ice-cream, such as an ice lolly and a choc bar, or a brick with wafers and a water ice.

Sleeping arrangements

As well as being grouped as a family at meal times, girls were similarly grouped in dormitories by Ma, for very specific reasons. 'I have known an epidemic of bad language to be caused by placing a little new girl, who arrived with a large vocabulary, in a dormitory with other little 10 year olds. That six 10 year olds should sleep together is a totally abnormal condition. When, therefore, I rearranged the dormitory with ages of 10, 14, 16, 18, the natural sequence followed, the epidemic slipped into the past as childish bravado.' This system meant that while the younger girls went to bed in the light, older girls had to creep soundlessly to bed in the dark. However, most of the 6th formers slept in *Retreat* and *Retreat Room*. Ann Early was given one of the small rooms as a study because she was excessively clever and hardworking. It was known as *Rosy Cottage* because Ann had such a pleasant nature. Several of the old girls said that the mixing up of age groups at meals and at night time really contributed to the feeling of family life at MG.

At the beginning of each term, there was a fire practice and girls had to evacuate their dormitories. *Balcony* used a ladder fire escape which had anti-burglar wires which twanged in the wind. *Big Room* and other rooms on the first floor had ropes which were hooked on to the window frames, and each girl had to slide down the rope, to land in the shrubbery. *Pond 1* and *2* and the other second floor rooms used special canvas sling seats, which many girls found quite a palaver and very nerve-racking. Mary Riley, for one, dreaded fire drill and had a fear of heights all her life.

In winter, girls collected hotwater bottles, *hotties*, from a lined wicker hamper at the top of the second staircase. This was replenished several times during the evening.

Sleeping out

Sleeping out, for the pleasure of it, was a highly prized privilege. Some girls slept out on the balcony, others used the verandah of the San. On summer nights, many girls slept out in the garden on old-fashioned folding wooden beds. When it rained, the girls had to grab their beds and race for cover in the entrance hall. Fifty years later, Ruth Behrens remembered the 'joy to lie on a summer's night listening to the nightingales and to awake to the dawn chorus.' Hazel Dodds too rated sleeping out as one of her best memories, with starry nights and owls hooting. Once she and a friend waited until they thought everyone would be asleep and crept down in their nighties to the bottom of the garden. There were two or three ropes hanging down from a big tree and the girls swung on them for a time, feeling very wicked indeed and loving it. Even in the war, girls continued to sleep out and this practice was only stopped abruptly when one girl woke up to find a piece of shrapnel on her pillow. There were ack ack guns on the Oxford Road and pieces of shrapnel were often found in the school grounds.

SCHOOL WORK

Bridget Luard reckoned that at the age of 13½ she knew four Shakespeare plays by heart and could knock up a rabbit hutch, but couldn't recite the 3 times table.

Miss Chambers' philosophy of school work was very avant-garde for her time. Girls coming to MG from other, more conventional schools experienced quite a culture shock.

For school work, the girls were put into small groups of six to 12 children. The Groups started at Group II and went up to the VIs. In the 1920s, the youngest Group had lessons in the garden

The senior girls worked at their own bureaux

cottage, a wooden building divided into two parts, school room and carpentry shop. Peggy Neal
Green was taught there in 1929, when she was 8, the youngest and smallest child in the school.
There were no toilet facilities and the girls had to rush to the main house through rain and snow.
Group V was the School Certificate Year and there was a very small Group V Remove for those
not taking the exam. Each Group had a Group mistress, whose business it was to discover the
capability of each individual. This was because Miss Chambers believed that, 'the finding of some
gift or interest in one particular field acts, like the turning on of a tap which pours courage into
the child to attempt work in other directions. When, by the lack of fear of punishment and by
complete intellectual freedom, freedom which is only gained by self-discipline, children will find
courage to carry out the things which are real to them and which matter, and to do the difficult
drudgery often necessary to attain the achievement of their desire.'

The general timetable, made for everyone, included plenty of free time for each girl's own
individual interests. In her first year, each girl based her own timetable on the general one, getting
clear what work she wanted to pursue for herself. There was no need for competition, Ma
believed in self-motivation and self reliance. 'The actual work of the school is based on what has
proved to be the natural taste of all children, with ample freedom for the child who diverges on
to lines of her own.' All work at the school was voluntary, and as Joyce Cutbush remembered,

'we could attend lessons or not as we pleased, allowing staff their private opinions of us if we failed to turn up. I believe I did miss one lesson, but on the whole we did not take advantage of this concession.' It was well known that Teresa Cripps spent a whole term without attending a single lesson, preferring to garden or read on her own. Nevertheless, she passed Oxford Responsions with flying colours.

Helen Robinson who came with her twin sister, Marian to the school in 1927 recollected that, 'we were known as "the school where they did no work", but in my year people went on to train in teaching, drama, medicine and two girls gained admission to Oxford to read for degrees.'

The times of lessons throughout the day were marked by the ringing of a pair of authentic cow bells. These were rung first at the top of *Stable Yard* and then in the main school building.

In Miss Chambers' words, 'The work of the lowest groups, and again at the top of the school, is more untrammelled than that of the group which take the School Certificate. It is in the work in the bottom of the school particularly that we find a real standard is acquired – the standard without which later work would be so hampered. Throughout the Lower School much of the

The school library

teaching is individual, we find this very marked in the teaching of history, geography, and science. In French, Latin, mathematics and music there is more demand for class teaching. As an example of the value of individual work, I would quote the achievement in geography of one small 12 year old, who devoted a whole year to studying the transport systems of the world – with the aid of travel agencies, steamship companies, ordnance maps and so on. Her four large maps, when completed, even included air-routes up to date, and camel tracks across the desert. Another girl, working individually in science, wrote and illustrated a complete scientific treatise on rodents. I quote these out of innumerable similar achievements as examples of the standard and finish which quite young children can attain. The accomplishment of this work gives so much more happiness than does the old convention of marks, competitions, and prizes.'

In history, half the time was given over to 'free work', when girls had the opportunity to make a book on a subject of their choice. A drama teacher, Audrey Lovibond, remembered a 12 year old girl compiling *A History of Writing* and achieving some beautiful script and hieroglyphics.

Bridget Luard reckoned that, at the age of 13½, she knew four Shakespeare plays by heart and could knock up a rabbit hutch, but couldn't recite the 3 times table. Oll Early to this day asserts that 'they never taught spelling at MG and you will find I never learnt it. In the 6th form, I spent a lot of time learning trigonometry and advanced maths with Miss Parry who tried to keep a page ahead of me. I had decided architecture would be a good combination of disciplines for me to study. After I qualified, I was surprised to find one of the Priestley daughters being elected to the RIBA at the same time.' Peggy Neal Green had problems with her lack of maths grounding when she went into the war services. She was commissioned as a navigator, but lacked any knowledge of geometry and one of her fellow officers had to give her the necessary coaching each night. When Cynthia Morris came from North London Collegiate School, class work at MG could not have been more different. 'Maths lessons seemed very babyish to me at the age of 12, mental arithmetic drills were absent, and we were taught tables with the aid of a special pack of cards as a sort of game. In class, I quickly got bored as I was not being introduced to new work. However, Miss Margaret Parry, the maths mistress, and Ma arranged that I should have a special weekly tuition session on my own, so that I could forge ahead with quadratic equations and geometry theorems.'

Work in Group VI was individual and specialized. For girls going to a university or taking music or art, the programme was mapped out. Most girls tended towards the arts in their choice of work, and there was greater inclination toward literature, music and art than to mathematics and its allied subjects. Girls who went to university usually took degrees in languages, literature, or history. Many girls, whether planning for a career or not, continued their education at music college or a dramatic or physical training college. Very few girls took mathematics or science. In her six years at MG, Mary Behrens could remember only two girls who went to study medicine and there were no aspiring lawyers, scientists or serious academics. By today's standards, the school laboratory was badly equipped and science teaching was very rudimentary. Cynthia Morris felt she was taught biology well and, in her group, most girls took it for School Certificate. However there were no structured lessons in chemistry and physics and those subjects were not taught to a reasonable examination standard. Girls with very high flying ambitions had to go to a crammer or college to get their Higher Certificate.

Despite its progressive stance, there was no sex education at the school – girls were left to sink or swim. When a girl began her periods, she had to get her sanitary protection from Matron. Ma would be informed, and then asked the girl to come and chat with her, but nothing was said ahead of time to prepare the girls for this tumultuous event. Cynthia Morris and Peggy Neal Green remember these sessions with Ma, but no further information on the facts of life was proffered. Despite having three sisters, when Peggy went into the services she thought if someone kissed her she would become pregnant. When she asked her mother how she could have let her daughters go away from home with so little knowledge, she was told that she had been given a book – all about fairies, birds and bees!

When Joyce Cutbush joined the school, the Board and the syllabus for School Certificates was different from the Board at her old school. 'I read some Shakespeare plays several times over and others, which I should have read, not at all. I loved literature, especially poetry, and was fascinated by history. I covered most of the history syllabus on my own as the teacher assumed I had already covered much more ground than I had. In retrospect I should have taken more advice as to what subjects to study as I dropped science altogether, even biology, which I now see as a great mistake. I did manage to scrape through Matric. with enough School Certificate Credits to qualify, but I think the examining board was being lenient, owing to war-time conditions.'

S 2   Dec.

OXFORD LOCAL EXAMINATIONS
SCHOOL CERTIFICATE
THURSDAY, DECEMBER 4, 1941
TIME ALLOWED—2 HOURS
Shakespeare, &c.

[You must attempt Section A, and EITHER Section B
OR Section C—two Sections in all. In Section A
answer the first question which is set on your
Shakespeare play, and TWO of the other three questions on that play—three questions in all on Shakespeare. If you are offering Section B, answer the
two questions on your book of poetry; or else, if you
are offering Section C, answer the two on your book
of prose.
Your answers must be given up in two separate batches,
corresponding to the two Sections. Remember
therefore not to answer any part of a question from
one Section on the same page of your answers as
a question from the other Section.
On each page of your answers to Section A write
SHAKESPEARE in the space allowed for Name of
Examination Paper; for Section B write POETRY;
for Section C write PROSE. Number the pages in
each Section 1, 2, &c.
The questions marked with an asterisk (*) should be
answered as fully as time allows.]

41 C 37   Turn over.

School Certificate papers, 1941

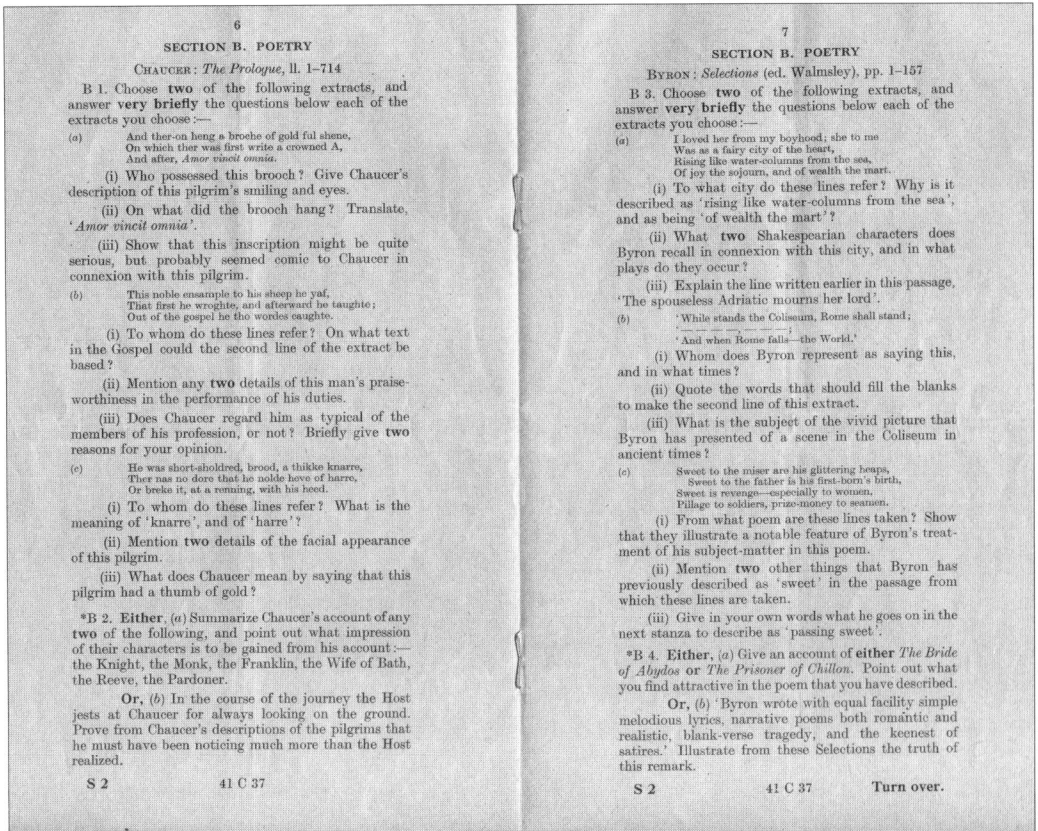

In the senior groups, once over the School Certificate hurdle, life was very civilised. Girls could wear their home clothes and there were extra curricula activities and instruction in dress-making, cookery and millinery. Girls had their own dress allowances and could buy or make their own clothes. These were not always a delight to the onlooker, but as Ma said, 'better to make your mistakes here'. There was a demand from girls in Group VI for tuition in more languages and modern history both European and English. In Peggy Neal Green's teen years, there was a General Election and John Cripps came to lecture the senior girls on the Labour Party ideas of his father, Sir Stafford Cripps. There was not a similar visit from a Tory – against Ma's liberal ideas perhaps.

The method of teaching at MG was certainly interesting

6

SECTION B. POETRY

CHAUCER: *The Prologue*, ll. 1–714

B 1. Choose **two** of the following extracts, and answer **very briefly** the questions below each of the extracts you choose :—

(a) And ther-on heng a broche of gold ful shene,
On which ther was first write a crowned A,
And after, *Amor vincit omnia*.

(i) Who possessed this brooch? Give Chaucer's description of this pilgrim's smiling and eyes.

(ii) On what did the brooch hang? Translate, '*Amor vincit omnia*'.

(iii) Show that this inscription might be quite serious, but probably seemed comic to Chaucer in connexion with this pilgrim.

(b) This noble ensample to his sheep he yaf,
That first he wroghte, and afterward he taughte;
Out of the gospel he tho wordes caughte.

(i) To whom do these lines refer? On what text in the Gospel could the second line of the extract be based?

(ii) Mention any **two** details of this man's praise-worthiness in the performance of his duties.

(iii) Does Chaucer regard him as typical of the members of his profession, or not? Briefly give **two** reasons for your opinion.

(c) He was short-sholdred, brood, a thikke knarre,
Ther nas no dore that he nolde heve of harre,
Or breke it, at a renning, with his heed.

(i) To whom do these lines refer? What is the meaning of 'knarre', and of 'harre'?

(ii) Mention **two** details of the facial appearance of this pilgrim.

(iii) What does Chaucer mean by saying that this pilgrim had a thumb of gold?

*B 2. **Either**, (a) Summarize Chaucer's account of any **two** of the following, and point out what impression of their characters is to be gained from his account :— the Knight, the Monk, the Franklin, the Wife of Bath, the Reeve, the Pardoner.

Or, (b) In the course of the journey the Host jests at Chaucer for always looking on the ground. Prove from Chaucer's descriptions of the pilgrims that he must have been noticing much more than the Host realized.

S 2   41 C 37

7

SECTION B. POETRY

BYRON: *Selections* (ed. Walmsley), pp. 1–157

B 3. Choose **two** of the following extracts, and answer **very briefly** the questions below each of the extracts you choose :—

(a) I loved her from my boyhood; she to me
Was as a fairy city of the heart,
Rising like water-columns from the sea,
Of joy the sojourn, and of wealth the mart.

(i) To what city do these lines refer? Why is it described as 'rising like water-columns from the sea', and as being 'of wealth the mart'?

(ii) What **two** Shakespearian characters does Byron recall in connexion with this city, and in what plays do they occur?

(iii) Explain the line written earlier in this passage, 'The spouseless Adriatic mourns her lord'.

(b) 'While stands the Coliseum, Rome shall stand;
—— —— ——
'And when Rome falls—the World.'

(i) Whom does Byron represent as saying this, and in what times?

(ii) Quote the words that should fill the blanks to make the second line of this extract.

(iii) What is the subject of the vivid picture that Byron has presented of a scene in the Coliseum in ancient times?

(c) Sweet to the miser are his glittering heaps,
Sweet to the father is his first-born's birth,
Sweet is revenge—especially to women,
Pillage to soldiers, prize-money to seamen.

(i) From what poem are these lines taken? Show that they illustrate a notable feature of Byron's treatment of his subject-matter in this poem.

(ii) Mention **two** other things that Byron has previously described as 'sweet' in the passage from which these lines are taken.

(iii) Give in your own words what he goes on in the next stanza to describe as 'passing sweet'.

*B 4. **Either**, (a) Give an account of **either** *The Bride of Abydos* **or** *The Prisoner of Chillon*. Point out what you find attractive in the poem that you have described.

Or, (b) 'Byron wrote with equal facility simple melodious lyrics, narrative poems both romantic and realistic, blank-verse tragedy, and the keenest of satires.' Illustrate from these Selections the truth of this remark.

S 2   41 C 37   **Turn over.**

to the staff. Ma was adept at choosing imaginative staff who shared her views on the need to break the mould of the usual school routine which was then available. The teaching staff were allowed to be individual and were invariably kind and helpful. Many old girls were very loyal to Ma and returned to teach at the school after university. Among these were Helen Robinson, Esther Salaman and Mamie Watson.

Apart from music, English was probably the best taught subject, and in the late 1930s was taught by Miss Fanchiotti, known as Fan. She was well-read and encouraging to girls who enjoyed creative writing. When Audrey Lovibond came to teach in 1942, she took a weekly English lesson known as *Fourteen Lines,* when each girl had to repeat at least fourteen lines (i.e. the length of a sonnet) of poetry of her own choosing. They often learned far more than that for the joy of it. Audrey was thrilled when she heard one of her class calling it 'our lovely lesson.'

After Miss Parry left the school in wartime, Miss Yule took over maths, biology and Latin teaching. Miss Yule was a conventional teacher; able and erudite, and she taught the pleasure of intoning Latin verse. She expected a lot from her pupils, but was quick to praise good work. Audrey Lovibond, who believed strongly in experimental teaching, was surprised to discover that some of the best results in the school were achieved by Miss Yule's more formal approach. Miss Yule also supervised and did a great deal

Miss Fanchiotti, the English teacher *(left)* **and Mrs Kingsley, Housekeeper**

of gardening, and took nature walks with the girls, which were very popular. 'I knew that her methods and mine would always be very different, but I came to respect and eventually to like her very much indeed.'

French was taught by Mlle Verchere, who was quite a martinet but an excellent teacher. She slept in a small room at the top of the main staircase. She had a high regard for hygiene and Mary Behrens remembered her always polishing her cutlery at meals before eating and giving her bath an extra scour! She used to walk round the school carrying her own little cushion with its loop in her fingers. German was taught by Mollie Kemp, known as Kempie, who favoured the direct method of total immersion, so no English was allowed in her classes for beginners. Holding up a pencil, her first words were, 'Das ist ein bleistift'. This system seemed to work, as the group studying German for School Certificate all passed with good grades.

Unusually for girls, there were carpentry classes taught by Mr Arrowsmith in a big wooden building in the grounds. He came weekly and tutored the girls in the rudiments of using a hammer, nails and a chisel. Pamela Neal Green made a chair. Cynthia Morris chiselled an ash tray and also made a small bathroom stool and a rabbit hutch. The routine creations were bureaux, which girls used instead of ordinary school desks when they were in the senior groups, and hutches for rabbits and guinea pigs in the school farm.

The carpentry shop – making a bureau

School reports

Reports were written on thin sheets of A4 card. At the very top, there was a space about 8" x 2". Until 1935, the girls devised lino-cuts to fill this space and one design, approved by the art mistress, was printed for all the reports. Later on, every girl produced her own picture to fit this space, to enhance the report for her parents. The art mistress was responsible for these headings and had to make time in her art lessons during the last few weeks of term for these to be produced and then stuck onto the report cards. The reports on each academic subject by the relevant teacher were the usual run of the mill, but as there was no testing, either during or at the end of the term, no marks were given. There were reports on the arts and crafts and music, Matron's report, a general house report and a general school report. The latter often included trenchant comments by Miss Chambers regarding academic progress and social behavior.

…needs to work harder. She is never idle but her mind is not occupied with the acquisition of knowledge. She is interested but does not tackle a subject with capacity.

…occupies herself well. She has worked independently at a variety of occupations.

…good at heart, but her actions and her point of view are often too childish, she would be so valuable if she could aim at wisdom.

…began the term with what might be called a superior attitude. There has been a definite improvement since half-term – she has been a nice, simple, helpful girl.

…must fight a growing tendency to a sharp tongue and to critical gossip. She is so sound of heart that both are beneath her own good feeling.

Ma's ideas of teaching through play are part of the Froebel tradition of teaching. Ann Roest, the niece of Tibbie Hardie, a former Matron, was a student in 1964-1969 at Bedford Froebel Training College for teachers, where 'Miss Chambers' work was quoted to us as of excellence.'

An example of a report heading, 1933

GIRLS TRAVEL TO SCHOOL ON	Thursday, April 25ᵗʰ	
GIRLS TRAVEL HOME ON	Thursday, July 25ᵗʰ	
ENGLISH	Marian is quick to understand what she reads; her written work is good.	EH
SCRIPTURE	Is interested but does not take much part in discussion	L.C.
HISTORY	Good - works keenly & well	E.M.H.
FRENCH	Satisfaisant	Y.R.
ARITHMETIC	Very good.	E.B.
SCIENCE	Marian works independantly, she has spent most of this term reading.	D.A.B.
GEOGRAPHY	Marian has covered far more ground this term: her work is much more finished	EH.
MUSIC [CLASS]	Promising.	D.W.
[PIANO]	Marian has made some progress. Her work would be satisfactory if she could avoid stumbling in performance	D.W.
DRAMATIC WORK	Marian must try to learn her parts more quickly. She is a spirited member of group plays	EH.
ART	Good	F.M.F.
POTTERY	Marian works well & keenly and is a great help in the Clay Room.	E.B.
DANCING	Good.	S.O.D.C.
GYMNASTICS	Good. very keen work.	S.A.M.
GAMES	very good - promising.	S.A.M.
CARPENTRY	Very good.	A.E.
MATRON'S REPORT	Marian needs rather much care - then she is very tidy.	

FREE WORK REPORT   A very capable worker.

GENERAL HOUSE REPORT   Good.

Grown 9⅞ 3″ ⅜

B. Chambers.

A school report, showing the range of subjects that girls were taught in the 1930s

MUSIC, DRAMA AND ART

The front hall of the school was decorated with laurel leaves and oranges and the smallest girls, standing on Hot Seat, played percussion instruments to accompany On Christmas Night.

Music

The school was remembered by many pupils as a place where they learnt to love and appreciate music, which played a big part in the school curriculum, and there was always the sound of someone practising an instrument.

Miss Ruby Holland, known as Rah, was Ma's companion and colleague. She was in charge of all musical activities, as well as teaching piano herself to selected girls with high music ability. She had been a promising pianist in her youth and had been on tour with a famous Italian singer, Louisa Tetrazinni. Evidently it was usual in those days for an aging diva to take a young hopeful to play the piano during the intervals. When Rah met Ma, she was in mourning for her boyfriend, who had been killed in World War 1. Ma explained she was founding a new school and wanted Rah to teach, but she replied, 'I am a performer, I don't teach in anyone's school'. Ma's reply was, 'That's just why I want you'. In the end, Rah made a great career at MG, teaching the piano, teaching music and conducting choral singing.

Ruth Behrens was one of Rah's pupils. 'We were told that Rah's piano lessons cost 6d a minute – 40 minutes cost £1 – and as a consequence I would be reduced to a quivering jelly of apprehension at every lesson, thinking that each mistake was costing my parents another shilling or so. Ma fed this fear by her efforts to encourage me to practise more fervently, telling me about the sacrifices my parents were making to send me to the school – "Your parents don't drive a car, do they? How many of your friends' families don't drive a car?" and I couldn't think of any.' Hazel Dodds was also one of Rah's pupils. 'She was an inspiring teacher, it was a great privilege to be taught by her. My discovery of what music was came when learning to play Bach's *2nd Piano Invention.*'

Most girls learned to play an instrument and two other members of staff taught music at the school, as well as there being various visiting teachers, including Enid Berridge, who had been one of the first pupils at MG. Miss Cummuski taught the piano and also took the younger pupils for band, in which they played triangles, cymbals, drums, recorders, tambourines, and bells. She often joined in with the music, playing the piano. Kempie was another piano teacher and also taught music appreciation.

Piano instruction was based on the *Matthay method* – arms had to be very loose and weighty while fingers were nimble. Lessons were given weekly, but practising was expected daily except for Sundays. A large practice timetable was drawn up, allocating practice rooms to each girl. The best room was Ma's drawing room which had a beautiful, baby grand, the next best was *Pond Meadow* on the first floor, which also had a baby grand and was used for music classes. This room was next to the dormitories, *Pond 1* and *Pond 2*. There was an upright piano in *Serbian Stripes,* one of the other dormitories, and an another upright in a room not much bigger than a large wardrobe, known as *Cupboard.* Girls with real music ability were given the best practice rooms, while those with average to low ability found most of their practising allocated to *Cupboard,* with perhaps *Pond Meadow* once a week. Mickey Jones was one of the school's most talented musicians. One term, when she was learning Bach's *Italian Concerto* and *Beethoven's Pathetique Sonata,* she would practise in *Pond Meadow* in the evenings. Sue Sanderson used to 'creep along the corridor in my nightdress in order to hear better, it was wonderful!' The Associated Board of the Royal Schools of Music awarded Mickey two gold medals, two years running. To celebrate this, the whole school was offered a choice of different outings to the ballet, the opera or Gilbert and Sullivan at theatres in London. Mickey later performed under the name of Michelle Carte. She played and broadcast extensively, both as a soloist and as a chamber musician.

Mickey Jones

By contrast, Cynthia Morris has vivid recollections of *Cupboard,* where most of her practice sessions took place. It was at the bottom of the wooden stairs which led to the maids' rooms, next to the two *Pond* dormitories. It was very claustrophobic, with just room for a piano and a chair, without a window. 'It certainly put me off piano practising! I was a very mediocre player but I did learn *Für Elise,* which my fingers can still remember 60 years later. I also had to play occasionally for the dancing classes, mainly extempore chords!' Dinkles Sanderson, who played a string instrument, had to practise in a class room before breakfast. The room was cold and often the room was still being cleaned. She recalled that 'it was torture'.

Classes in music appreciation and music theory were held at least twice a week for third formers onwards. In 1937, there was a weekly radio programme on understanding music which the music class listened to for part of their lesson. The construction of a symphony was one of the themes, and different instruments of the orchestra was another.

Joyce Cutbush remembered, 'I loved music appreciation with Kempie. Either when I was still at school or soon after I left, I went to my first operas, *Madam Butterfly* and *Queen of the Night*. I also went to my first symphony concert in the old Queen's Hall, shortly before it was destroyed in the bombing. Sometimes, recitals were held at the school, to which outsiders were invited. I had the privilege of showing Harriet Cohen, the pianist, the way to the loo!'

MALTMAN'S GREEN.   CAROLS.   CHRISTMAS 1935.

In Dulce Jubilo   arranged by Pearsall
Joseph Dearest, Joseph Mine. Vaughan Williams.
——————————

Christmas Eve.   Traditional German.
Lullaby of the Christ Child. Old French.
Joy to the World.   Handel.
——————————

Song of Praise.   Brahms.
The Shepherd and the King. John Wilson.
Herrick Carol.   Martin Shaw.
——————————

The Christ Child.   Rathbone.
——————————

Noel.   Maurice Besly.
When Joseph was awalking Sarson.
——————————

The Dream of Christmas   Holst.
One Wintry Night.   Hunt.
——————————

Sleep Holy Babe.   Dykes.
A Christmas Carol.   Reinecke.
——————————

Cradle Song of the Virgin. Barnby.
Gabriel's Message.   Basque Carol.
The Coventry Carol.
——————————

What Child is This?   Traditional.
On Christmas Night.   arranged by V. Williams
——————————

Christmas carols programme, 1935

Rah's choice of choral music was quite ambitious for such a small school. It included works such as Pergolesi's *Stabat Mater*, Bach's *St. Matthew Passion,* and *The Peasant Cantata*. Groups were mixed up in these sessions, there was no audition for the choir, and not all the girls had perfect pitch! The choir also sang part songs and madrigals, such as *The Silver Swan*. The choir performed at the Summer Term Open Day, either in the gym or in the garden if the weather was fine.

In the Autumn Term, carol singing was popular, and unusual carols were often chosen, which were not always in published form, so singers had to write down the notation in their manuscript books. The annual carol concert, organised and conducted most professionally by Rah, was the highlight of the year, memorable for girls and parents alike. The front hall was decorated with laurel leaves and oranges, and the smallest girls, standing on *Hot Seat*, played percussion instruments to accompany *On Christmas Night*. The carol, *What Child is This?*, was usually part of the programme. *When Christ was Born* by Reineke was sung in two parts, not only musically, but physically as well. The choir was divided, one half singing from the ground floor and the other from upstairs, in the corner of the gallery outside the Sick Room. Sue Sanderson found that the King's College Christmas carol service was the only one 'which brings me as much delight as the MG carols,' and hoped that *the Reinecke* would one day be included in their repertoire. The Christmas party also included carols. As a finale, a conga-like snake of girls formed, depositing each girl to her dormitory on route, accompanied by the carol, *The Holly and The Ivy*.

Drama

Mamie Watson was a pupil of MG, who came back to teach English and drama after leaving Oxford. Here again, the girls were lucky enough to be getting professional tuition, since she was a Saint Denis producer. She drilled the girls to her own impeccable standards, and Sue Sanderson, who played Lucia in *The Comedy of Errors* and the Shrew in *The Taming of the Shrew*, loved every minute of it, despite Mamie's fierce instruction. Mamie was full of ideas for plays, 'inspirational' was the description given by many of the girls. Some of the plays which she produced she had written herself. The standard of plays, production, stage management and acting was very high, and Ruth Behrens thought, 'the knowledge that a number of girls had parents who were stage professionals, spurred us on.' Girls not keen on acting could contribute to the ambitious plays produced each term, by designing, making and painting scenery. The costumes, too, gave an opportunity for creative work. Elizabethan costumes were both machine and hand-sewn by girls from their own hand-designed and hand-printed materials. Annette Ingold had a particular flair for this, which led her to a career in the history of costume.

I hold the world but as the world...
A stage where every man must play a part

Maltman's Green
Christmas 1935

Christmas card, 1935

At the end of term, there was the Saturday Play Day. Groups of different ages performed full length or one act plays to an audience of parents. In winter months, plays took place in the gym, where a series of long benches of different heights was arranged for the audience. In the Summer Term, plays ranged from *Winnie the Pooh*, in which Peggy Neal Green played Piglet, to *Alice in Wonderland,* where a real live piglet took part and ran wild throughout the seated parents! There was usually Shakespearean comedy performed in the garden – weather permitting. Plays included *A Midsummer Night's Dream*, where Peggy leapt out of a cedar tree to put a girdle round the earth as Puck, *As You Like it, Love's Labours Lost,* and *The Taming of the Shrew,* where Petruchio was played by Jenny Ramage. Jo Dodds was another girl whose acting was remarkable. J. B. Priestley, the well known novelist and playwright, used to come to the plays and take off his jacket to show his red braces! He did not always think very highly of the dramatic productions, and Hazel Dodds remembered him making rude comments!

After Mamie left MG, she studied under Reinhardt and became very much part of the theatrical world. She lived in a flat overlooking the Thames and when she was very ill with cancer, her flat was always full of flowers and distinguished visitors, such as Laurence Olivier.

Art

Art was taken by Miss Hodgkiss in the art room. Girls were allowed much free expression and poster paints were often used. In those days, a set of six poster paints cost 6 shillings. Sue Sanderson remembers the paints drying out and losing much of their colour. She used to get the Dryad catalogue and save up for some special materials or equipment. In her last term, she bought a spinning wheel and was able to display some spun wool in the Summer Term's exhibition. 'It was always a delightful challenge to try to put up a better show than the year before.' Girls who showed a real talent in art were given the exclusive use of a little studio for serious painting, upstairs above the classrooms facing the gym. It must have originally been the corn store as there was a corn shute in it! Sue Sanderson, Sylvia Priestley and Boo Behrens were among those awarded this privilege.

The art room off *Stable Yard*

Pottery (not an extra) was also on the timetable, in what had been the Drummond's greenhouse, off the stable yard. It had a grape vine on the roof with big bunches of green grapes in the summer. Miss Cook (Chef) was in charge and the girls produced some innovative work.

The pottery room with a grapevine growing inside

HEALTH, EXERCISE AND GAMES

'In the morning, girls had to lie in bed in their dormitories until Matron or her assistant had come round with a mugful of thermometers to take everyone's temperature. No-one could get up to wash or to go to the loo until then.'

Miss Chambers' written pronouncements about health and well-being in *The Modern Schools' Handbook* are somewhat meagre – 'Games, gymnastics, and dancing, and, in the Summer Term, swimming, though not compulsory, form part of the day's work, and Matron and the games mistress combine to exact some form of fresh air outing and exercise daily. In the matter of health, and especially when young, the girls may not have that freedom which they enjoy in other directions, and are in this respect in the hands of Matron and the Housemistress.'

When the school was founded in 1918, the worldwide flu epidemic was just over and both teachers and families of pupils would have suffered losses of relatives and close friends. Health was considered of great importance and in closed communities, such as boarding schools, there were always fears of epidemics and illness. Helen Robinson, who was at the school in the 1920s, remembered a girl who fell ill, went home and then suddenly died. The whole school was shattered by this experience. Another girl had diabetes and everyone knew that she would not survive until adulthood.

Of 28 schools advertising in *The New Statesman and Nation* in 1937, nearly half mentioned the importance of health as a key inducement to prospective parents. St Christopher's School offered an 'open air atmosphere'; Wychwood School claimed that the 'health of the school (was) exceptional'; Croham Hurst School boasted its 'healthy and beautiful situation'. MG's reference to health was 'Gerrards Cross is 300ft above sea level and is on gravel soil'– good drainage obviously considered of paramount importance!

Ma was a great believer in fresh air and pupils with bad chests slept out of doors, whatever the season, as this was thought to be a very healthy practice. Like the Drummond family, some girls slept on the balcony, but they had the benefit of a shelter hut. Others used the verandah of the San. A heavy storm sheet was hooked across this in bad weather. Peggy Neal Green remembered pouring the contents of her *hottie* on to the snow from here when she was about ten years old. Lois Hambly, one of three sisters at the school, slept on the roof outside *Balcony* for several years.

Balcony was a popular sleeping place

During the 1930s and 1940s, the various Matrons must have built up quite a list of health dos and don'ts for the girls in their charge, some of which look distinctly eccentric in the 21st century. Matrons remembered were Isobel Hardie, (Tibbie), Anne Johnstone's mother, (Mrs Johnny), Miss Freestone (Frasty behind her back), followed by Miss McCullough (Mucky). The latter two Matrons were efficient, but feared! Then came Mary Green (Mogs) who was plump, cheerful and easy to get on with. She was followed by Miss Townsend (Towny) and Miss Hughes, (Suzie) – both of whom left to get married. By 1937, there was an acting Matron, Miss Deane (Deanie), and of course there were numerous assistant matrons who came and went. In early 1939, a recent school leaver, Peggy Neal Green, was invited by Ma to come back to the school as assistant matron as a war job. She regarded this as an odd choice, since she had no medical training. Her duties, however, were mainly handing out medicines, dealing with coughs and colds and communicating with the Doctor, calling him in if need be. She felt she really could have done with more training, as the lack of it showed when one girl had an epileptic fit while waiting to go to the air-raid shelter one night. Although she managed to get the girl into the office, she did not know what to do next and had to call for help.

In the morning, girls had to lie in bed in their dormitories until Matron or her assistant had come round with a mugful of thermometers to take everyone's temperature. No-one could get up to wash or to go to the loo until then. During the first three weeks of term, temperatures were taken at tea-time as well. The idea behind this was to catch anyone with a fever and isolate her before anyone else in the school caught the infection, in the hope of warding off any epidemics. Breakfast was followed by gargling. Girls queued up by the back stairs with their white enamel tooth mugs for a horrible carbolic tasting mixture and then went into the bathroom to gargle. Ruth Behrens even remembers having to sniff salt and water up her nose (one nostril at a time) in an effort to nip sickness in the bud. Peggy Neal Green stopped *temps* and gargles after the first three weeks of term.

However, when Cynthia Morris had a high temperature one morning, she was thought to be malingering. 'I really felt quite ill, shivery and hot in turns, slightly sick with a terrible headache. A thermometer was put into my mouth

Girls queueing up for their gargle

and, when the assistant matron looked at, it she accused me of having put it onto the radiator and told me to get up. I dressed and tottered downstairs, but when I got to the dining room, I fainted. The next thing I knew I was in the San. I had had a very high temperature and had some variant of the flu. I was in bed for a week and then, once I was up, I was so weak that I was excused all lessons. Since it was summer, I just lay on my rug in the garden and read and slept all day.'

One day, Boo Behrens cut her knee badly and the doctor stitched it up without any analgesic. She developed a fever and a rash, and was rushed to the sick-room with a dettol soaked sheet hung over the door. She had some sort of scarlet fever, a nasty illness in the pre-penicillin days termed *Surgical Scarlet*. As a precaution against an epidemic, all her books and toys were burned!

Girls with bad colds were mostly isolated in the San and occasionally isolated in single rooms in *Retreat* dormitory. Joyce Cutbush remembered being given a 'red sausage' – a gelatine capsule of red granules – which she found difficult to swallow, and a change of pyjamas in order to sweat out her cold. Girls on outings to London always had to suck a prophylactic cough sweet to ward off London germs! In the four years 1937 to1941, there were no epidemics at MG, so the regimen of lots of fresh air, gargling and temperature-taking must have paid off.

At the beginning and end of term, girls were weighed and their height measured. Girls who had lost weight the previous term were considered delicate and given brown bread honey sandwiches in Matron's room at tea-time after games. Ultra-violet rays were given to girls prone to coughs and colds. Twice a term, girls were given a foot inspection for athlete's foot and veruccas. Girls with flat feet did various exercises in the gym, twice a week before breakfast, to raise their arches; one of these was walking along an upturned form, trying to pick up pieces of cloth with their curled toes.

There were no antibiotics or even antiseptic creams in the 1930s. Stinging iodine was the norm for cuts and grazes. Girls who fell down on the hard courts in games frequently had bits of grit in their knees. The cure for this was a dreaded hot fomentation, where lint was immersed in boiling water, wrung out, and applied to the knee, which was then bandaged up. One day, this happened to Cynthia Morris and the pain from the fomentation was quite unbearable. When she undid her bandage, she found to her horror that the fomentation had raised first-degree burns blisters on her knee. No more fomentations after that experience!

GENERAL HOUSE REPORT.   *Marian has grown 3" and gained 2 lbs this Term.*   *Good. 4'7⅞"*

Changes in height and weight were noted on school reports

Games and exercise

There was very little formal gym on the parallel bars and horse, unless the weather was very inclement. On fine days, girls were taken out to the nearby common and spent their time running up and down the dells, playing tag and hares and hounds. When it snowed, the girls went tobogganing down the slopes.

Dancing was a weekly activity and was very free style, termed *Central European*. The girls wore an assortment of silk tussore dance tunics in pastel colours and danced to music in the gym.

In the summer, girls played tennis and the juniors also played rounders. Tennis matches were held against other schools. In the 1920s, when Mary Behrens was in the MG team, a team arrived from another school in long white dresses, sunbonnets and long cotton stockings. The MG team usually wore their tunics but on this occasion, as the weather was sweltering, asked to play in their shorts. Most girls went swimming, but as MG did not have its own pool they were transported to an outdoor unheated pool at *The Bell*, a road house, on the Oxford road, much used at weekends by the general public.

Ma had the idea it was bad for growing girls to lean over a hockey stick so, in the Autumn and Spring Terms, netball and lacrosse were the school team games. New girls were mystified when, soon after the start of term, they were given a lacrosse stick and inducted into the art of greasing the leather netting to make it more supple – a very boring and rather horrid occupation. Lacrosse practice was usually at mid-morning break, when there was a rush and scramble to put on lace-up lacrosse boots before going to the games field across the road from the school. There were formal lacrosse games in the afternoons. Because the school was so small, it was not too difficult to be chosen to be in a team. Cynthia Morris, who was hopeless at games, once found herself playing first home in a school match. Hazel Dodds and Dorrie McMurray, who were no good

(left to right) **Jean Harper, Peggy Pearson, the games mistress, and Joyce Murray**

at games either, often found themselves put in 'goal' and hated having hard balls thrown at their unprotected faces. Joyce Cutbush was also dragooned into playing goal and was not allowed to wear her spectacles, in case they broke. Eventually Dorrie insisted on having a horse at the local stables, so that she could ride twice a week instead of playing lacrosse.

Most of the girls remembered having a weekly practice game with a team from the Slough Ladies Lacrosse team, or *Sluff Hags*, as they were known at MG. The players were thought to be frightfully old, but the matches were always good-natured and friendly affairs. Dorrie was mystified that an adult would wish to play lacrosse out of choice!

Ruth Behrens, who was in the team, felt that matches with other schools were always played bravely. 'We had only one team, whereas many of the schools we played against had many to choose from. Sometimes we found ourselves playing against 2nd or 3rd teams, who were amazed to hear we were the only team. But out of an entire school of only 60 girls or so, we couldn't have more. We were glad when we won, but the non-competitive attitude of MG put matches in a much more relaxed light and I can't remember ever bothering much whether we won or not. This attitude was reiterated by Dinkles Sanderson, who at the end of one such match, saw that the defences were exhausted and puce in the face with effort, while the attacks were frozen.

'We did feel a keen sense of individuality and a pride in our somewhat eccentric school character – and I'm afraid were inclined to look askance at other more conventional schools. This difference was brought home to me very strongly once during the early days of the war. We were due to play a school near Beaconsfield one Saturday afternoon. There had been an air-raid alert and our transport had not turned up. A Harrods van had been delivering food to the school and was obligingly going in our direction, so we hitched a ride in it. The host school was a very formal establishment and the school team was lined up in the drive, standing to attention with their lacrosse sticks when this van arrived, spilling out a group of giggling MGites in a very dishevelled state. The hosts were not at all amused, whereas we considered the event the most tremendous lark, and we found it difficult to take the match at all seriously from then on.'

After games, the girls always had to change their vests and leave their old ones in their personal locker in the big airing cupboard outside *Serbian Stripes* dormitory before changing into mufti for the evening. Girls who were were not playing games put on their coats and galoshes and in groups of four could go for walks in the surrounding fields or down to the village.

FREE TIME AND LEISURE ACTIVITIES

'Sunday is by general consent the favourite day of the week. The girls have come to regard it, entirely of their own accord, as a different day – a day to be set aside for all the pleasant things for which there often is not time during the week.'

Miss Chambers wrote, 'The girls have much free time for their occupations, though the tendency, especially about the age of 14, is to pack too many into each day. These activities range through the care of their pets at the farm, the making and mending of hutches and other equipment for their animals, weaving, carpentry, pottery, jewellery, and every form of handwork, and the making of stage properties, scenery and clothes.'

Pets

In the 1930s and 1940s, children were allowed to keep animals in the farm near the back drive, which had a wooden hut with sacks of oats and bran for feeding the animals, hay for the hutches and a water standpipe. The pupils kept bantams and ducks (there was a pond), rabbits and guinea pigs. There were also some geese which the girls, to their shame, sometimes teased.

Pets included rabbits and ducks

Girls made their own rabbit hutches in carpentry class

Miss Chambers judging the rabbit hutches at the farm

Girls were not allowed to keep a rabbit until they had made a hutch for it in the carpentry shop. The hutches had wire runs and sleeping quarters and were built with strong handles, so that they could be lifted and moved to new patches of grass when necessary. The roof lids were hinged or removable, covered with rain-proof tarpaulin. Great inventiveness went into their construction, with sliding floor sections that made them easier to clean. Some girls even made collapsible, portable hutches, so that they could take their pets home in the school holidays.

In the morning before lessons began, donning galoshes and, sometimes, raincoats, girls with pets rushed to the farm to feed and water their animals. They carried hot water from the kitchen in billy cans to make warm bran mash. In Cynthia Morris' second year, she bought a white rabbit for 3s 6d and borrowed a hutch while finishing her own in the carpentry shop. When her rabbit was full-size, it was mated, became pregnant, and produced five baby rabbits, which were quickly earmarked by various friends. Unfortunately, wild rabbits also abounded and as the hutch was moved from one patch of grass to another, the little rabbits caught myxomatosis and all of them eventually died. 'This was my first experience of life and death and was quite traumatic. I gave away my hutch and no longer went to the farm.'

Ma kept an ancient black spaniel called Jill, which accompanied her everywhere round the school. Whenever a girl had a birthday and a birthday cake, a slice was always put on a plate outside the drawing room for Ma. However, everyone knew that the cake was really for Jill. One day Jill ate a candle and the order went out that no more candles on birthday cakes were allowed!

Weekends

It was Ma's view that, 'Their leisure the girls can spend as they choose, and weekends prove to be the most profitable part of the week from an educational point of view. Sunday is by general consent the favourite day of the week. The girls have come to regard it, entirely of their own accord, as a *different* day – a day to be set aside for all the pleasant things for which there often is not time during the week. On Saturday evening, they may organize an impromptu play or a party, and the day will be taken up with preparations for it, but on Sunday, until the service at seven o'clock, nothing claims them, and, even at that, their attendance is voluntary.

'Church going is entirely optional. Very often a party goes off to church, or a few girls may walk across the fields to Jordans Meeting House, sometimes a party may go up to London to a service at St. Martins-in-the-Fields.

'Always on Sunday morning, there is a roll-call, when each girl gives in her name and the places where she may be found during the day. This is done more to prevent vagueness in the girls' own minds than for the sake of keeping a check on them. For the rest they are free to do what they please: to visit the farm; to work in the clay-room or the carpenter's shop; to practise; to work in the laboratory; to garden; to do their handwork. Sometimes, parties of girls start off on an all-day walk, taking a picnic lunch with them, provided that they have made all their arrangements beforehand, so that neither cook nor housekeeper have been inconvenienced. There may be a few bad managers who do not use their weekends well. Naturally, it takes some time and experience to learn how to spend leisure wisely, but the children, starting young, readily learn how to manage their work, so that they are left with time for the pursuit of their own particular interests.'

Entertainments were held on most Saturday nights, when each Group took it in turn to produce their own play or games. Ruth Behrens remembered some visiting entertainers, called *The German Singers* (who may well have been a group of German refugees), who demanded much audience participation. 'I walked back to the station with them, singing German folk songs en route. Miss Clark was another visitor, a superb storyteller of the old school – some of whose stories I remember to this day. Occasionally, we were allowed to listen to broadcast concerts, but any other listening (especially to dance bands) was frowned upon. The bathroom attached to *Retreat,* my dormitory, was next to the housekeeper's room. I remember lying in the bath, with my ear pressed against the thin partition, listening with delight to Henry Hall or Geraldo! Forbidden fruit indeed.'

One of Cynthia Morris' most vivid memories of a Saturday night entertainment was of Esther Salaman, a large woman with magnificent tawny hair and a wonderful voice, singing some of Hilaire Belloc's songs, *The Chief Defect of Henry King, Matilda,* and others.

In the days before television, Joyce Cutbush and friends spent much of their leisure time reading or preparing and performing impromptu sketches, 'one a skit on western movies in which, dressed in my home-made siren suit, I was a cactus flitting by, shuffling from one side of the stage to another to great amusement.'

Mary and Ruth Behrens

A lino-cut of *sloshing*

An unusual summer pastime at MG was *sloshing*. This was a traditional 'privilege' that in retrospect, seems the sort of practice one should avoid. But it was eagerly awaited, as it meant the arrival of high summer. The girls gathered in *Stable Yard* and, two at a time, stripped off and washed from head to toe in a bucket of cold water. Then, standing against the wooden gate, buckets of water would be thrown at them – one bucketful at the front and one at the back. No squawking was allowed. Even a genteel squeak would result in the banning of *sloshing* for the rest of the term, so it was all done in deathly silence, but with many grimaces.

Peggy Neal Green enjoyed walking across fields in a group, 'crossing the railway lines we put halfpennies on the tracks, hoping they would squash into pennies, but they never did. Returning, we could pick wild strawberries along the banks.' Breakfast walks in the summer were a great pleasure to Ruth Behrens. 'We had picnics in woods and fields that were easily accessible from the side of the garden. I loved these walks. On Sundays, when we chose to go to some form of worship, I walked across the fields to Jordans, the Quaker Meeting House, where the roof was made from beams of the *Mayflower*. I eventually became a member of the Society of Friends.' Hazel Dodds also enjoyed walking to Jordans, which had a very peaceful atmosphere, and grew to admire the Quakers very much. Joyce Cutbush shared the same sentiments. 'I still value silence as an essential part of worship and spiritual growth.' Sundays were rounded off with a short, informal choral service. The girls sang *Jerusalem* and *God be in my Head*. There was a reading from the Bible by one of the girls, (Hazel Murray, who had a strong voice, was often chosen for this), and a story, such as *The Little Prince* by Oscar Wilde, or *The Grumpy Saint*, read by Ma.

On Monday nights, the school often gathered in the drawing room to sit on the floor to listen to *Monday Night at Eight* on the radio.

Outings

After the First World War, girls went to the Cenotaph in London on Armistice Day each year. Other, more enjoyable, trips to London were also arranged from time to time. Girls were able to see Old Vic plays, with parts taken by now legendary actors, such as John Gielgud, Laurence Olivier playing Macbeth, Peggy Ashcroft as Juliet and Edith Evans as her nurse. When there was a particularly interesting Shakespeare production, the girls went to see it. Dinkles Sanderson saw the best *Midsummer Night's Dream* of her life in Oxford, directed by Max Reinhardt.

A large party of girls went to the Centre Court stands at Wimbledon each year to watch players, such as Perry and Austin, or to wander to other courts. There were frequent visits to the Queen's Hall in London and, later, to wartime lunch-hour concerts at the National Gallery, with soloists such as Myra Hess and Louis Kentner. Joyce Cutbush and Cynthia Morris went to these concerts and also to the ballet, which became a lifelong addiction for both of them.

Ruth Behrens remembered how MG celebrated national events in its own way. 'When the Duke of Kent (fourth son of George V and Queen Mary) married Princess Marina of Greece, we had a lacrosse match – the teams being the *Georges* (who wore cardboard crowns) and the *Marinas* (who wore Marina green ribbons in their hair – a fashionable colour of the time.) There were also special treats at the time of George V1's coronation.'

At half-term, some girls went home while others were not able to do so. Ma arranged for the half-terms to be fun and girls moved out of their dorms and went into tents or the attics to sleep. They had wonderful meals outside, could wear their home clothes and in the summer went to the *Bell* roadhouse for swimming.

Senior girls congregated to sit, chat or read in the Senior Common Room. This rectangular room, which led from the library, was furnished with armchairs and settees. There were black lockers round the walls with brilliantly-coloured horses painted on them, one for each member. Membership was by invitation only, mainly for girls in the 6th forms. Some studious girls from the 5th form were invited, and Cynthia Morris and a friend were the first of their group to enjoy this privilege. The lower groups had the use of a room on the *Retreat* corridor and this was usually very untidy and noisy.

The girls enjoyed various crazes. One year everyone was on stilts walking all over the gardens. Another outdoor pursuit was inspired by Sylvia Priestley's visit to American rodeos, and she initiated a game whereby the girls held small blocks of wood in their hands and then cantered on all fours over the lawns, even indulging in low jumps! Yo-yos were popular when they first appeared in the 1930s. Following on from Knucklebones, Jacks was another enduring indoor pastime, and the click of jacks on the group room linoleum floors was incessant. There was also a word game, called *Are you in Cahoots?*, played in Ma's drawing room some evenings. There was a trick answer to this, and if a girl got this right, she was no longer considered a new girl.

WAR AND THE END OF AN ERA

In the dining room, entire window frames hung outwards as though on hinges, all the windows having been blown out by the blast, just one original pane of glass remaining.

The war brought all sorts of changes and the pre-war pupils did not always find the changes agreeable. They felt the old school as they knew it begin to fade.

Staffing

There was a very competent war-time staff. Miss Barker, the Deputy Head, was a tower of strength to everyone in her gentle way. Miss Yule, who taught maths and Latin, had come to MG to be with her mother away from London and the bombs. Helen Robinson, an old girl, was invited back to MG in 1940 to teach history and art and stayed for two years. She vividly recollected two girls, who stayed for only a short time at MG, who had escaped in a cargo ship from the south of France, and were en route to the USA. In her art class, one of them painted a seascape of colour and sunshine, while her sister painted a scene of a threatening storm.

However, war brought teaching staff shortages and senior girls found themselves involved in more responsibilities – supervising the younger girls at prep and checking on their black-out in the dormitories and bathrooms. The French teacher, Mademoiselle Verchere, left and evidently managed to return to La Rochelle in occupied France, to be with her elderly parents. It was at this period, too, that Ma's health began to deteriorate, as the medication and gold injections she had been taking for her very painful arthritis began to take their toll. Peggy Neal Green, the assistant matron in 1939, was very close to Ma and saw how her health and mind were failing. 'Ma became vague. When I visited her each morning in the flat, she would still be in bed. I ignored some of her orders, that seemed odd to me. Nothing was to interfere with the school.'

The domestic scene

The numerous maids who did the housework, cleaning the dormitories, classrooms, bathrooms, and kitchen, all left to go into munition factories and, as permanent domestic staff were difficult to find, the girls had to take over some of the lighter housework duties. Mrs Dunkerley, a large formidable woman, reputed by the girls to have once been a prison wardress, was appointed as cook/housekeeper. She was in charge of the domestic scene and the rotas, which ensured that each girl did her daily communal stint of housework.

In the bathrooms, as a war-time measure to save fuel, each bath had a black line painted well below the taps, which indicated the allowed ration per bath of about six inches of hot water. As well as their usual bed-making routine, girls now also had to mop and dust the dormitory linoleum floors daily, and presumably the floors were wet-mopped regularly by the domestic staff. Classrooms too were dusted and mopped by the girls. Mrs Dunkerley had high standards and berated girls who did not do housework to her satisfaction. Joyce Cutbush hated the housework. 'I always felt giddy when I stood up after sweeping up the dust. In 1943, when my father was temporarily in the army, my mother was at a loose end and was invited by Ma to come to MG for a short time to help out.' Mrs Cutbush had many a stint on the sewing machine, turning worn sheets from sides to middle.

She also helped in the vegetable garden, as fruit and vegetables were in short supply. In fact, one day, girls were asked to pick nettles to be cooked! It was difficult keeping the gardens going, because all the gardeners had been called up, save Philip Taylor, a general *boots* factotum, whom Mrs Cutbush found cheery and who helped with her barrowloads of weeds. Joyce Cutbush enjoyed this period, as her mother was able to take Joyce and various friends for the occasional day out to Windsor.

Meals

Once rationing was in force, meals probably were more spartan than previously. Mrs Dunkerly specialised in hot, filling puddings, such as jam sponge-rolls and spotted dick. When war began, there were no staff available to serve at table and girls queued for their meals at a hatch. There was no self-service. Mrs Dunkerly and a helper filled the plates, but they tried to be sensitive to the likes and dislikes of each girl, giving only the size portions which the girls thought they could manage. If girls tended towards plumpness, second helpings were frowned upon. After meals were over, girls had to clear the tables and then take turns in the washing up rota.

Sleeping arrangements – air-raid shelters

Just before the war started, air-raid shelters, with roofs of corrugated iron covered by a mound of earth, were built at the back of the school by the tennis courts. When the war began, girls were asked to opt either for sleeping in the shelter or staying in the dormitory and had to stick to their choice each night, come what may. The shelters had rows of bunks and uncomfortable, lumpy, straw mattresses, and the girls slept in sleeping bags – but at least when the raids started, the girls could stay put, a blessing on a cold winter's night. Some girls opted to sleep in the dormitory, because after trying out the shelters, they found them too claustrophobic. These girls slept in *Big Room* and wore siren suits over their pyjamas, made like Winston Churchill's in a cosy wool jersey material with a zip up the front. After the war, the shelter was used as a paint and tool store and was only cleared away when the new gym was built.

Maltman's Green
Gerrard's Cross
Bucks

Gerrard's Cross 3022

12th Sept. 1940.

Dear Mrs Overton,

A Mistress will be at the 4.15 p.m. train from Marylebone on Thursday, Sept.19th, to escort the girls to Gerrards Cross. If owing to the exigencies of the situation parents wish girls to be met elsewhere, or to send them by another route, we shall do our best to help them. High Wycombe station is only nine miles away from here. It is also possible to come by coach from Oxford.

We have had a number of air-raid warnings here, as elsewhere, and one bomb was dropped in a field about five miles away some time ago. This is the only trouble there has been anywhere in our neighbourhood.

Parents who would like their children to sleep in the air-raid shelters will be glad to know that I am having bunks fitted and special ventilation arranged for. The shelters will be thoroughly heated out every afternoon to avoid any damp which might come from the concrete. I should be glad if each child could have a nice warm air-raid suit, a very old eiderdown sewn up like a sleeping bag, and a very old pillow or cushion. Girls with outdoor sleeping things can use them.

Many of us still sleep in our own bedrooms as usual. I shall be glad to know if any parents prefer that their children should do this.

Yours sincerely,

p.p. B. Chambers

War memories and the landmine

Occasionally, the girls watched dog-fights overhead during the Battle of Britain. Ruth Behrens described the scene, 'I saw a fighter falling slowly to earth, in a tail spin, like an autumn leaf, totally out of control.' Invasion was threatened, one of the dates given being the day girls were due to take their School Certificate music oral. Instead of worrying about the progress of the war, the girls parochially worried lest the sound of gunfire and rumbling tanks would cause difficulties in the exams!

One night, in November 1940, near the end of the Christmas term, Ruth Behrens was one the girls sleeping in the shelter, and Cynthia Morris, one of the girls sleeping in Big Room, when there was a huge explosion. The Germans had jettisoned their spare bombs on their way home from heavy raids on Birmingham and Coventry and a parachute landmine dropped close to MG. It had drifted across the area and landed on Brittany, a house in Maltman's Lane, at the other side of the lacrosse field.

The house was flattened and nearby houses, including MG, were damaged by the blast. Two students from the Swedish Physiotherapy College in London, who had been billeted in the house after being evacuated from town, were killed. One old lady, who was blown out of her bath, was brought from her house in Maltman's Lane to Peggy Neal Green. Peggy wrapped her in a blanket and made her comfortable in the music room until the ambulance came, while everyone else went to the shelter in case of further bombs. Peggy owned one of Ma's puppies, and the dog and its bed were blown right on to her by the blast.

After the landmine fell, there were some bizarre sights. The curtain that hung behind the front door was draped over the grandfather clock in the hall. The large, gleaming copper urns that stood on chests in the entrance hall were dented like partly deflated footballs. In the dining room, entire window frames hung outwards as though on hinges, all the windows having been blown out by the blast, just one original pane of glass remaining. There was glass everywhere so everyone was packed off home or to friends. Many girls left, some never to return. Ma arranged for some of the London-based girls to go home with friends who lived in the country. Girls who lived some distance away stayed on for a few days, but the school was so badly damaged, that they couldn't use the group rooms, which were cordoned off. The girls wore coats and mittens indoors all the time, but their spirits were very high.

Ma made abortive efforts to find alternative accommodation in a 'safe areas', and toured Wales, Shropshire, Yorkshire and the Lake District to find a large house for the school, but failed to come across anything suitable.

Hobgoblin nor foul fiend
Can daunt his spirit :
He knows, he, at the end
Shall life inherit.
Then fancies fly away,
He'll fear not what men say,
He'll labour night and day
To be a pilgrim.

John Bunyan

The last years of Ma's era

MG opened in the Spring Term of 1941, following the landmine. Joyce Cutbush was one of the pupils who returned and took her School Certificate at the local centre in the summer. She did not realise at the time how difficult it must have been for Ma and the rest of the staff. Freedom had to have limits, with the likelihood of bombing or even of a German invasion. There were only 28 girls, enabling Ma to give the girls much of her attention. The hub of the house was her drawing room, where girls regularly gathered for talks, on subjects such as American history, considered important when Britain was anxiously waiting for the USA to enter the war. Play readings became a feature of Monday evenings, with works by Shaw, Priestley and Barrie.

In 1942, Audrey Lovibond came to MG as drama teacher. At first, she enjoyed the life. Classes were small and the girls were all prepared to be interested. But far from being 'free', the school was entirely under Miss Chambers' autocratic rule. Audrey Lovibond was aware that Ma had been a brilliant educational pioneer and had been impressed at her interview by Ma's forceful personality. But she soon began to find Ma disconcerting. The hypnotic power Ma had over girls could be very alarming. She continually interfered with her staff and might summon a teacher, in the middle of a lesson, to a lecture on something quite irrelevant. By the Summer Term, she had become most erratic and, one afternoon, upset a number of children. Audrey Lovibond and the art mistress consulted the family doctor about Ma's behaviour. When Ma heard about this, Audrey Lovibond was asked to leave and all of Rah's persuasive powers were needed for Ma to provide a testimonial for her. It was the end of Ma's era. Two years later, age and infirmity had so changed Ma's personality that she had to retire into a home, where she died in 1945.

CHAPTER THREE

MISS
LOWE'S
ERA
1945–1957

The House itself has never been able to make up its mind just exactly what it wanted to be like – – –

it runs up a few steps–

and out  of windows,

and in at doors –

and down a few others –

and round a pillar, till it arrives back at where it started from, and then it begins all over again.

– and along passages,

MALTMAN'S GREEN IN TRANSITION

'In 1948, the academic freedom previously enjoyed by MG pupils was curtailed by Miss Lowe and attendance at lessons became obligatory. She herself taught English and her attitude to school work was unlike that of Miss Chambers.'

After Miss Chambers went into a home in 1944, the School Council became responsible for Maltman's Green and, as a temporary measure, continued the work of the school under the chairmanship and guidance of Miss Holland, who also continued to teach singing and choral work. Miss Bull was Headmistress for a very short period.

In 1945, the School Council issued a statement on the policy of Maltman's Green, which gave due weight to Miss Chambers' ideals and educational theory: 'It is still our aim to provide such a school until the gap between theory and practice can be bridged by the implementation of the Butler Education Act of 1945 and its successor, and the special advantages of this school be extended to all.' These advantages were listed as:

"Firstly, the community life of a small boarding school with a staffing ratio of approximately 1 to 7, from which we obtain more observations of individual characteristics and therefore more possibility of securing individual happiness, and freedom from psychological difficulties. In this lies the possibility of the child's freeing herself from her own difficulties and so establishing her personality and developing her powers to the full.

"Secondly, the special opportunity for creative work in small groups, which gives the opportunity for greater freedom in both choice of work and in discipline. More creative work and greater freedom in choice formed one of the most important parts in Miss Chambers' theory of education, and it is our desire to help girls to live a creative life as members of a community."

In 1945, a new Headmistress, Miss Theodora Lowe, age 46, was appointed. She came originally from Robin Hood's Bay, on the north Yorkshire coast, and had an Oxford degree. She was a small woman, who kept her hair in a bun and usually wore high-heeled shoes and dark clothes. She had previously taught at Harrogate College, a small school of about 50 pupils, aged 7 to 18.

Mary Riley, one of Ma's last pupils, had enjoyed MG's progressive freedom when she first came to the school in 1944. Her aunt had been a friend and fellow teacher with Ma and Rah and had probably recommended the school to her parents. 'I had been fortunate in imbibing sufficient of the artistic aims of Miss Chambers and Miss Holland to give me a love of art, music and drama which has been a tower of strength throughout my life.' The MG personal ties to her family continued, as Miss Lowe was Mary Riley's god-mother.

In 1944, lessons were still not compulsory. Mary Riley spent her first term at MG painting in the art room under the eye of Leary, the art mistress. She and her friend, Betty Hadley Jones, were at MG during the difficult transition period in 1945, when Miss Lowe first took control of the school. It was a time of strikes, led by a quartet of girls – Anne Byam Shaw, Sylvia (Dickie) Bird, Hazel Adeley and Celia Gold, who were loyal to Ma's regime and refused to bend to new rules and regulations. The senior girls remained rooted to their chairs when Miss Lowe entered a room, refusing to stand up as she demanded. Miss Lowe was not able to instill her Harrogate College ideals until the two upper forms had left the school.

In 1947, Mary Riley was withdrawn from MG and sent to Harrogate College to be nearer her mother, while her father was abroad. The College's repressive regime was a nightmare for her. Five bad marks were punished by a silent meal in the school library – Mary ate there most Sundays! She was also ill for much of the time and confined to the San. Luckily for her, a consultant physician advised her mother against the northern climate and she was able to return to MG in 1948.

THE VERY TRUE BEGINNING OF WISDOM IS THE DESIRE OF DISCIPLINE; AND THE CARE OF DISCIPLINE IS LOVE; AND LOVE IS THE KEEPING OF HER LAWS.

MALTMAN'S GREEN.   CHRISTMAS, 1946.

The school Christmas card, 1946

In 1948, the academic freedom previously enjoyed by MG pupils was curtailed by Miss Lowe and attendance at lessons became obligatory. She herself taught English and her attitude to school work was unlike that of Miss Chambers. She encouraged those who produced good work, but expected high standards from all her pupils and was critical of girls whose work failed to reach these standards. Although showing interest in every girl, her prime concern was exam success. The girls took examinations at the Chalfont St. Peter's Convent – all of them passed, many with matriculation.

Some old MG practices continued. Girls were allowed a strip of garden if they wished and, although the farm was no longer in existence, they could keep white mice as pets. Carpentry was still included in the curriculum, but pottery had been discontinued for ten years. In the 1950s, Nora Kay, a local potter, was instrumental in making pottery an extra subject. She had just started up as a freelance artist after teaching full-time in the Art and Technical School in High Wycombe. She was looking for a workshop and a friend suggested she should try MG. After an interview with Miss Lowe, she was offered the use of the old school pottery for a modest rent, to use for her own work both in term time and in the school holidays. Miss Lowe was delighted to be able to add pottery to the curriculum for an extra fee, of which Nora Kay received a percentage per pupil.

The old greenhouse, still with grapevines under the glass roof, was in a dirty, chaotic state, with only the bare necessities still in place. There were low benches, a table, some stools, a sink and a cold tap, slatted shelving, cupboards and a clay bin. Other useful implements were found – jars, pots, bowls, buckets, boards and rolling pins. The cupboards were full of rotting bags of clay which had to be thrown away and re-ordered. The old wooden kick wheel had acquired a wobble, which made it a lethal trap for fingers, so a new wheel was bought.

After a summer making everything ship-shape, pottery classes began in the Autumn Term.

There were two classes a week for six to eight children, which took place after 4.00pm. The girls were given roomy smocks to wear over their uniform since, to start with, some turned up in their ballet clothes or riding gear! Nora Kay found that pupils became interested once they could create pinch pots and moulded dishes, but heartily disliked the preliminary, necessary clay wedging, pleading, 'can't you do this for us?'.

Both pupils and staff seemed to regard the pottery as a free-for-all. Staff looked upon it as a good place for girls to paint scenery, devise costumes and do any other activity that might make a mess. Girls also used the pottery in unscheduled hours, opening the cupboards and leaving the benches, the wheel and tables dirty. This was solved by securing the cupboards with stout cord and immobilising the wheel.

An old gas kiln had been discovered in a shed in the garden. When there were enough pots for a firing, this was put to the test. It was a nightmare, because the furnace spat flames and roared. When it was opened, revealing disappointing results, Nora Kay decided to ask Miss Lowe for a small electric kiln. Although Miss Lowe agreed to the installation of a new kiln, the school refused to pay for it, and the cost was deducted from Nora Kay's rent payments!

Eventually, there was enough glazed pottery to have a small show at the MG summer garden party and this was judged a success. From then on, there were increased numbers of pupils and the classes became easier to run and teach.

Drama

On Saturday nights, one Group or other provided entertainment for the rest of the school by performing an impromptu play – a *Saturday Nighter*. This was the highlight of the week and occupied the whole day for the group of girls taking part. There was a wonderful costume wardrobe kept in a huge cupboard in the classroom used for the youngest girls.

Drama also continued to be an important part of school work. Each summer a play was performed in the garden for parents. The school was full of the offspring of theatrical parents, hence the high standard of plays. One year there was a performance of *Toad of Toad Hall*, with Celia Gold as Toady and Paula Wheatley–Dyson as Ratty. Another year there was a production of *Tobias and The Angel*. Mary Riley played the blind Tobias and practised her part by walking around blindfolded!

The standard of music teaching continued to be high under Rah's guidance. Girls with rooms in *Retreat* remembered listening to the older girls practising their piano pieces - Shirley Barnes and Jenny (a god-daughter of Bernard Miles) were particularly good performers.

Leisure activities still included performances by visiting artists. There was a regular visit from a string quartet and various singers, including Esther Salaman, who gave Meg Macaskie and Mary Riley a love of opera. After leaving MG, they both went into the props department of the Carla Rosa company. Eventually, Meg left to go to Glyndebourne and Mary got married.

After the war, theatre visits resumed. In 1948, Mary Riley wrote to Alec Guinness, having seen him in *Richard II* at the Lyric Theatre. She was then invited to meet him backstage and asked Miss Lowe for permission to see another performance with Betty Hadley Jones, Shirley France and Dutchy Van Lennop. Miss Lowe agreed, on condition she was included in the party.

Girls could still walk to Jordans, take tea in the *Pond Tea House* in Chalfont St Giles, and go for outings with their parents to *The Bull* or *Ethorpe*. Happy times were spent in the Senior Common Room sitting round the fire telling stories, while munching *Clinker* bread baked hard in the oven. When the first TV arrived at MG and was installed in the drawing room, all the girls crowded in to watch a film starring Gracie Fields.

The carol service, as ever, was a great event and the school spent the whole of the Autumn Term preparing for it under Rah's tutelage. At the Christmas party, Father Christmas would read a poem about each pupil, many written by Miss Lowe herself.

However, other aspects of MG changed. Miss Lowe thought that some of the home clothes worn by senior girls were outlandish and too extreme, so senior girls had to continue wearing uniform like the rest of the school, although when there were parties, she allowed the girls to wear ear-rings and lipstick, neither of which would have been condoned by Ma.

Miss Lowe was a religious woman and instituted daily morning prayers. Girls remember her sailing in, her black gown flowing behind her and a pile of books under her arm. The old weekly Sunday evening school gatherings in the gym were discontinued and were replaced by Sunday evenings in the drawing room, where Miss Lowe read to groups of girls while they did their knitting or needlework. Hymns, such as *Abide with Me* and *The Day Thou Gavest,* were also sung.

Sunday was a relaxed day. Sometimes, a group of girls would go to Windsor for the day. Church-going was still not compulsory and girls could go to church as and when they wished. Some girls wandered over the fields to Jordans, others went to the Baptist Church. Miss Lowe, and some of her distinctive flock of girls in their purple uniforms, attended St James' Church in Gerrards Cross. There, she caught the eye of Derek Elliot, a fellow church-goer, who wooed and won her. They married in 1957, and Miss Lowe left MG after 12 years as Head. She retained her connections with the school by coming to the Christmas and summer plays. In the 1970s, her two great-nieces joined the school as boarders. She died in Cornwall, aged 88, in 1989.

CHAPTER FOUR

MISS
BURKE'S
ERA
1958–1978

SCHOOL CLOSURE BID
Parents fight speculators

Parents and Headmistress versus powerful bank in
SCHOOL TAKEOVER BATTLE

Now it's up to you, Minister

Parents plan to take over Girls' School
BID OF £10,000

Minister rejects bank's appeal

Victory for the girls of Maltman's Green

MALTMAN'S GREEN BECOMES A PREPARATORY SCHOOL

Like the old MG, the educational ethos was to continue to give girls a broadly-based education. The girls started French at 9 and Latin at 11. They were able to take German and Spanish as extras.

After Miss Lowe resigned, Miss E. Hobson was appointed Headmistress in her place, in April 1957. Unfortunately, her tenure was short. Ill-health compelled her to resign after only two terms, at the end of the same year. Miss Paula Burke, who had been teaching English and drama at MG for four years, was appointed Headmistress in January 1958. She held a teaching diploma from the National Froebel Foundation.

Peter Ewen, the owner of Maltman's Green, and Miss Burke then proposed a radical change to the school. Instead of taking girls up to the school-leaving age of 18, they decided to change the school into a preparatory boarding and day school for girls from the ages of 5 to 13. The girls would be prepared for Common Entrance examinations into senior schools. Miss Burke then wrote to all parents of existing pupils, as well as to the Ministry of Education, informing them of this change.

The changeover took place gradually over 18 months. Miss Burke kept on fully-qualified staff for the senior girls, who stayed at the school until the end of the school year in July 1959, and arrangements were made for those who wished to take 'O' and 'A' levels. The school then became an educational trust and was recognised by the Ministry.

When Miss Burke took over, there were 24 girls at the school and 13 staff. Jane Stockwood in a newspaper article about the school, showed that the old MG ethos still continued, with girls learning to be self-reliant and considerate of other people.

Teaching and education

Girls were prepared for Common Entrance examinations, from 11 to 13, for the large girls' public schools – including Roedean, Wycombe Abbey, Cheltenham Ladies' College, Benenden, Sherborne, Queen Anne's, Caversham. The first scholarship was gained for Kingsbury School, Leamington. The educational aim was to continue to give girls a broadly-based education. The girls started French at 9 and Latin at 11. They were able to take German and Spanish as extras. Because of the demands of senior schools, they were taught both new and traditional maths, and were grounded in the new system of practical weighing and measuring. 'What the brain does not remember, the hands do,' was Miss Burke's credo. There was still a strong emphasis on the arts with dancing, class singing, drama and art and handicrafts. Extra subjects were ballet, learning a musical instrument, pottery and riding. A new system of streaming was introduced, so that a girl who was good at English was put in the A stream for that subject, but might be put into a B stream for maths. Miss Burke disapproved of prizes and competitions. For a few years, she organised an Open Day where parents joined their daughters at their lessons. In art classes, Pauline Hodder initiated the parents into the art of screen-printing or clay modelling.

Times of day were still marked by the ringing of authentic cowbells and it was the privilege of the Group III, 7 year olds, to take turns ringing the bells, walking all round the school.

As in Miss Chambers' era, each school report was headed by a coloured picture. This involved the art teacher in a lot of work, encouraging the children to produce their pictures in the art lessons, which were later pasted on to the reports.

Miss Burke divided the school into four Houses named after national heroes – Drake, Scott, Raleigh and Shackleton. The children were awarded plus or minus marks for their work and behaviour, and the total went to their house. There was an inter-house swimming competition and a competition for the best entertainment given by a house to the school. The house with the most marks at the end of term was rewarded with a party the following term.

The uniforms remained purple – purple dresses, coats and cardigans, with navy gym tunics, grey sports jerseys and corduroy slacks.

CRISIS FOR MALTMAN'S GREEN

With an eye to the main chance, the Bank realised that the 13½ acres of land were immensely valuable and, as trustees of the property, decided not to renew the lease in 1965, as it wished to use the land for a major housing development scheme.

During the first four years of Paula Burke's headship, the number of pupils rose from 24 to 120 – 40 of whom were boarders. As well as expanding, the school became successful in its new role as a preparatory school, with girls gaining entrance to many major public schools.

However, in 1962, problems arose over the land and building. Miss Burke was asked if the school would lend land for the construction of a swimming pool, so she approached the Chairman and principal shareholder of the school, Peter Ewen. He, in turn, wrote to the landlords, the Royal Bank of Scotland, which held the estate in trust under the will of Captain

Drummond, who had sold the building to Miss Chambers. The Bank sent a surveyor, who then consulted the lease. He discovered that the Bank had an option to break the lease in June 1965, which was unknown to Mr Ewen and Miss Burke.

With an eye to the main chance, the Bank realised that the 13½ acres of land were immensely valuable and, as trustees of the property, decided not to renew the lease in 1965, as it wished to use the land for a major housing development scheme. Plans were submitted to Buckinghamshire County Council, on January 31 1963, to develop the land for building 80 to 100 houses.

Mr Ewen, the principal shareholder of the school, decided not to oppose this planning application and instructed Miss Burke to close the school. He had previously rescued the school from financial disaster in 1950 and again in 1958, and did not feel prepared to accept any new loss. Furthermore, even if planning permission was not obtained, the landlords could greatly increase the school's rent from £500 to £2000 a year, because the property had been revalued under the rating assessment from a rateable value of £430 to £1600, which would present considerable financial problems.

Miss Burke knew of these proposals for a year before informing the parents. It must have been a very difficult year for her, while she tried to find a building in the vicinity large enough to house the school. She even looked outside the locality, in case there was one large enough to continue with boarders – taking in some of local day girls as boarders. As a last resort, she was prepared to amalgamate with another preparatory school. None of these possibilities proved viable and, eventually, on January 24 1963, Miss Burke wrote a letter to all the parents, outlining the position. Her final paragraph read, 'I am desperately sorry that (this situation) should have arisen. I know only too well what we are doing to your children. Had I known this situation might arise, I would never have started this preparatory school only four years ago.'

The reaction of the parents was shock, coupled with immediate action. They quickly held a parents' meeting, where they formed a Parents' Association and elected a Committee under the chairmanship of Mr J. Van den Bergh, whose daughter was in her last year at the school. Bunny Charters, the school matron with a daughter at the school, described the scene. 'Paula Burke stood up in front of her extremely critical audience and told the tale simply and with immense dignity, facing them all with her head up, and spoke evenly and with no false sentiment. At the end, there was a stunned and age-long silence. Then someone stood up and asked a question. She answered it and the ice was broken. The meeting became more and more enthusiastic and more and more questions were shot at her. She answered them clearly, and tirelessly. Then one of the parents stood up and said how much they admired Miss Burke and that no blame could be attached to herself in any way. That was the turning point. Mr Van den Burgh introduced a light touch and took the Chair. Paula moved back, but was brought forward. Never in our wildest imaginations had we envisaged such a response, since then she has had letters and phone calls saying how much they had admired her.'

A fighting fund was started to oppose the Bank's development proposals and any others that might be attracted to develop the property for profit. Subscriptions were collected and soon enough money was raised to open negotiations with the Royal Bank of Scotland. The Committee examined the whole situation and was confident that the school could be kept open and its future settled permanently on a sound business footing. Its intention was to form a Parents' Trust which would own and control Maltmans's Green. In an update to the parents, the Committee outlined Miss Burke's position. Since she was currently a director and employee of the Company holding the current lease of the school buildings and grounds, she was in a difficult position with regard to taking action in the school's future. However the Committee felt that, as parents, they wanted to stop any interruption to their children's education and wished Miss Burke to remain Headmistress, when the parents gained control of the school's future. Indeed, Miss Burke's continuation as Headmistress was considered essential to the continued progress of Maltman's Green.

Battle with the Royal Bank of Scotland commenced. Not only did Miss Burke and the parents oppose the scheme, but Chalfont St Peter's Parish Council opposed it, too. A petition was signed by a large number of local residents, who were also against the building plans and Buckinghamshire County Council refused outline planning permission.

The trustees had to prove in court that there were valid reasons for terminating the lease. The Bank's case, given by Eric Blain, Q.C. was that Maltman's Green was in a derelict condition. In particular, the surveyor, Mr A. Clapham, stressed the danger of a 'brick-built sewage plant in bad repair.' Serious breaches under the covenant were also alleged, because the grounds had not been maintained in a good condition. There appeared to be some merit in this complaint. The grounds had certainly not been kept up as they had been under Ma's reign. In an article for *CPA News* in June 1989, long after the affair, the part-time pottery teacher, Nora Kay, described the grounds when she had first arrived, in Miss Lowe's time. 'The run of the grounds still retained some feeling of a country estate. An overgrown, walled fruit garden, where I could find a few plums, apricots and raspberries; neglected orchards; sunny corners sheltered by lilac, and roses spilling over slopes, where one could have a lazy picnic.'

The other evidence given was that fire escapes were inadequate and Mr Clapham stated,

'I was absolutely horrified by those two iron ladders, which were the only means of escape. There should really be a proper staircase – not a ladder.' Evidence given by Mr R. E. Megarry, QC, counsel for the school, strongly refuted these criticisms and strenuously defended the condition of the school. Miss Burke gave evidence that recently 'in darkness, during a fire practice, complete with two fire engines – the school was emptied and hoses were on the roof in four minutes.' One of the witnesses, Miss Lillian Charlesworth, Vice President of the Association of Headmistresses, said she was amazed to hear such criticism. After inspecting the school, she had found the premises 'highly suitable'. Plans for improvement and modernisation of the school were outlined by Mr J. Van den Bergh. To enable the school to cater for 160 girls, new classroom accommodation and a hall were to be built.

On January 9, 1964, the Buckinghamshire Advertiser blazoned across its pages, *'Victory for the girls of Maltman's Green.'* When the application by the Royal Bank of Scotland for high density housing was turned down, an appeal was heard by an inspector of the Ministry of Housing at Whitehall. The Ministry, in its turn, also refused the bank's proposals. It is fascinating that the Bank was so unaware of the strength of the opposition to its plans and was defeated because of the quite undisguised, but different, agenda of three groups in defence of the school.

On behalf of the parents, Mr Van den Bergh said, 'I am only taking an interest in this because I think the area needs a school. Because of the expansion of Gerrards Cross, it is essential that we have a school of this kind.' In fact, there were no other similar schools in the vicinity which could cater for the 130 girls at Maltman's Green. The 437 local residents objected to the Bank's plans, because they wanted to retain the pleasant ambience of the area and abhorred the idea of high density housing near to where they lived. The third group was the County Council, whose

Saving Maltman's Green

spokesman, Mr H. Astley, felt that the site of the school should be retained for educational purposes. 'This school forms a natural buffer between the residential development and the Green Belt.' But he did go on to say, 'The council might want this site for itself, if the present school should cease to exist.' His view was supported by the assistant area planning officer, Mr S. M. Palmer, who said, 'The local education authority needs a site in this area for a secondary school – and this site would meet that need.' But he added that the existing school already served a 'very definite local need.'

By the Autumn Term 1963, an arrangement had been made with Mr Ewen for the Parents' Association to take control of the shares and to take over the running of the school. In 1972, there was a three day visit from Ministry of Education Inspectors and the school was granted an Alpha rating. In 1978, fifteen years later, the freehold of the land was acquired and Maltman's Green was safe at last.

CALM AND CONSOLIDATION

The atmosphere continued to be warm and homely for boarders and the very young children were happy and comfortable. On the first night of term every boarder had not only a goodnight kiss but a gobstopper. 'One cannot cry with homesickness while sucking a gobstopper.'

Now that the future of the school was assured, Miss Burke was able to develop Maltman's Green with energy and imagination. In this period, a solid foundation was laid for academic subjects and music, drama and art continued to develop as important parts of the school curriculum.

School uniform continued to have a purple focus. In winter, girls wore purple coats and grey hats. Indoor uniform consisted of white blouses, grey pleated skirts or grey corduroy or nylon trousers, and purple cardigans. In summer, girls wore cotton dresses in lavender and yellow checks, navy blazers and round straw hats with purple ribbons. Their outfit was completed by white cotton gloves, which were de rigeur for bidding farewell at the end of the school day.

School work

The broad-based education on the arts side now had to accommodate more science teaching. The Common Entrance examination to a large extent dictated the syllabus. Up until 1974, the exam had two optional science questions in a General Paper, which many of the girls chose to answer. Despite there being no laboratory, science teaching for girls of 9 and upwards was already well-established. The young, enthusiastic teacher, Jill Lewis, taught science in classrooms using a science trolley. This had two Bunsen burners powered by a Calor gas cylinder, a sink and a tap which pumped water up from a big plastic container below, adjacent to another container which caught the waste from the sink. The classrooms used for science were upstairs and the trolley lived in the upstairs corridor, lined with padlocked cupboards full of equipment and chemicals needed for teaching. The trolley was unwieldy to move, as each classroom doorway had a step, but children were always willing to help wheel it wherever needed.

When Wendy Wilson came for interview to teach science and nature study in 1974, she was put out to hear that there was no laboratory, but then cheered to hear that a purpose-built laboratory was to be included in the new classroom block. She was asked to design this, which she did with the help of the Head of Science from the prestigious Pilgrims' School in Winchester, who gave her a copy of their new laboratory plan and a list of essential equipment. Dr Desmond Hall, the school doctor and governor of MG, agreed that the laboratory should be equipped to the highest standards. It had five service and work-stations around the edge of the room for practical work, as well as tables for sitting and writing. Each work-station had a sink, two Bunsen burners and an electric plug, circuit boards, microscopes and other equipment. The girls worked in small groups of three or four, so that each girl could participate. The new laboratory opened in 1975, just in time for the new separate science paper introduced into the 12+ and 13+ Common Entrance exams, based on the new Nuffield science course. This had questions on chemistry, physics and biology. Once a year, there was an Open Day with a hands-on science exhibition, where visitors could try their hands at experiments set up by the girls.

Good use was made of the school grounds for nature study. Girls went pond-dipping for tadpoles, and gathered specimens from the hedgerows and wood. They kept tadpoles and caterpillars and watched them metamorphose into frogs and butterflies, which were then returned to the wild. The girls also went for nature walks into Siblets Wood, as well as being taken on field trips and to museums further afield.

Music and drama

Music continued to be taught well and girls participated in lessons and performances with enthusiasm. Boarders who learnt an instrument practised before breakfast in the various practice rooms throughout the school. The two *Bosendorfer* boudoir grand pianos, which used to grace Miss Chambers' drawing room and *Pond Meadow* music room, were still in use and looked after with good care. In 1975, Miss Burke appointed Shirley Massey as teacher of class singing throughout the school. Her colleague, Anne Wilson, was in charge of class music and recorder classes. Summer theatrical performances in the garden had been a long tradition, and many of these now became musical events. One example of this was a musical version of *The Twelve Princesses,* in the mid 1970s, performed in the grounds with a cast of 240 children. The original fairytale was turned into a play by Paula Burke's father and Shirley Massey composed the musical choruses. Miss Burke wrote her own libretti for Christmas performances and asked Shirley Massey to set parts of these to music. In 1977, their first full-length musical, *We're all going to Bethlehem,* was not only performed by MG pupils, but also by a London church drama group, as well as being recorded – a tremendous success.

Miss Burke organised afternoon sewing parties for mothers to make costumes for the Christmas performances and, in the summer, to make costumes for the plays held in the grounds. Fathers, too, were cajoled in helping to erect the staging.

Art

Pauline Hodder was Head of Art from 1968 to 1990. She had previously worked in the industrial and commercial art world, which gave her a wider range of knowledge, experience and interests than most conventional art teachers. She established a structured programme for teaching art throughout each year. The girls started lessons in the art room from Group III. In various stages

*Maltman's Green
has much pleasure in inviting you to
"We're All going to Bethlehem"
on Saturday, 10th December, 1977
at 3 p.m.*

R.S.V.P.

**An invitation to a performance
of** *We're all going to Bethlehem*
and some of the performers

Girls wore red, green or blue sail-cloth smocks in the art room

over the next five years, they learned simple rules and factual methods in working with various media. Subject matters were general and one year's theme for exhibition was focussed on life at MG – lessons, happenings, customs and traditions and food. In Group IV, the emphasis was on colour and light. 'Colour games were always most popular – staring at a square of colour, then at a blank space and seeing its ghost. Surprise and delight at making green shadows with a red light and blue shadows with a yellow one.' Then came the development of abstract work, the feel for composition, and the printing of repeat designs by various methods. Girls in Group VI had more varied activities – drawings, lino-cuts and model making.

Physical Education

Ten years after Miss Burke became Head, she approached Patricia Journet to teach PE. She was very well-qualified, having Diplomas in Theory and Practice of Physical Education from Bedford PE College and London University. She was undaunted by the limited facilities for sport – the assembly hall, which served as a gym, had very little equipment; the swimming pool was in process of being built; and netball, tennis and junior games took place on a rough surfaced area.

There was no competitive sport nor matches held against other schools. But Pat Journet found that latent talent and enthusiasm abounded and, as it was summer, made a start with swimming. The Dixon family kindly allowed the use of their own pool three afternoons a week, in which beginners and promising swimmers had lessons. A year later, the school's own outdoor pool was completed and every girl in the whole school had a swimming lesson every day. In the evenings and at weekends, the children had supervised fun in the pool. Soon the school was competing against other schools within a 15 mile radius, and winning many matches.

In the Autumn and Spring Terms, the swimming teams had training sessions at Amersham swimming pool, and later at Chalfont Leisure Centre. Wycombe Abbey School also kindly lent the use of their pool. Miss Burke initiated the IAPS Swimming Gala at Stoke Mandeville Hospital and the Maltman's Green teams were always among the winners of the Under-10, Under-11 and Under-13 events. In 1970, every girl in the school took part in a big swimming display. By now, not only diving but also synchronized swimming was featured. Music was provided by a piano on the pool-side, played by a member of the staff until taped music and underwater equipment became available.

Other sports were practised, such as badminton, hockey, rounders, and volleyball, but there was an obvious need for a new gym for the girls to reach their full potential.

Boarding

The atmosphere continued to be warm and homely for boarders and even the very young children were happy and comfortable. On the first night of term, every boarder was given not only a goodnight kiss but also a gobstopper. 'One cannot cry with homesickness while sucking a gobstopper – and they were large in those days.' The children had a fairy post box in the grounds where they could post letters. These were collected by the groundsman and taken to Paula Burke, who always made sure they were answered. Sometimes, a child wrote because she had not heard from home recently and then Matron would contact the child's parents or send a postcard herself. The *Fairies* also left a 6d piece, 'with wings', under a child's pillow if a milk tooth had been put there.

There were 12 dormitories, named *Pond 1, Pond 2, Serbian Stripes, Day Nursery* (shades of the dorms in Ma's day) *Pond Meadow, Heffalump, Wolery, Tigger, Eeyore, Kanga, Roo* and *Zoo*. None of the dormitories held more than eight children. Every bed had its quota of soft toy animals and the bathrooms were decorated with cheerful print curtains and fish. There were common rooms for seniors, juniors and babies, each of which had comfortable seating and books and even a doll's house for the younger children. The young children were read bedtime stories by staff or older

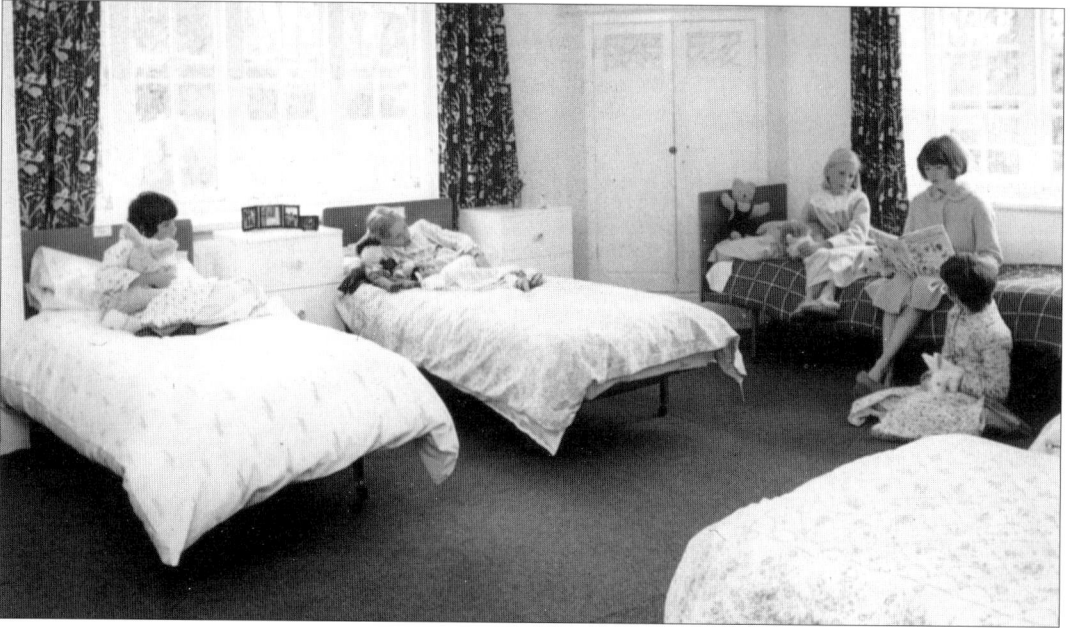

Girls in _Zoo_ dormitory

girls. Day girls as well as boarders were each given a 'shadow', another girl in their group, who helped them settle down and showed them the ropes.

Boarders were allowed small pets, such as rabbits, hamsters, guinea pigs and gerbils, which lived in the animal house. Once, a large run was put on the grass outside the art room for hamsters, but this was abandoned because there was a surfeit of them! The girls fed and watered their pets and cleaned the hutches. One new parent, on seeing the pets, asked if her daughter could bring her pony, but this was refused.

There was a party atmosphere on Saturday nights. In winter, games, such as _Hide and Seek_ and _Sardines,_ and treasure hunts were played all over the house. In summer, games were played on the lawns and the old lawn tennis courts, often ending up with supper on the grass. Once the swimming pool was built, girls swam and played games in the water. As the evening wore on, the younger children were sent up to be bathed, but came downstairs again for milk and biscuits.

Sunday evenings were also special and known as Miss Burke's evenings. A short service was held with moral stories before supper. The girls then went to the drawing room, where they played quieter games, such as _Pass the Parcel, Spelling Bee_ and _I-Spy._ At about 8pm, the older children were allotted a 'baby' each to take upstairs, wash and put to bed. Then they themselves got into their night clothes and came downstairs in their dressing gowns to sit and chat.

The Fours' common room

Bunny Charters, the Matron, made a list of girls' birthdays at the beginning of each term. She said, 'Miss Burke asked each girl what kind of cake she wanted and, on the nearest Saturday, the birthday girl had a party for her own group and any sisters from another group. She was also given the privilege of using the front-stairs for the day. This started a tradition to see who could run up and down the stairs the most times and beat the record. When the record reached more than 100, this became too exhausting and was discontinued.'

On Saturday mornings, Matron held mending classes for the boarders. 'By the time they left for senior school, I expected the girls to know how to darn, sew on buttons, hooks and eyes, mend seams and put up hems. It was a pleasant, gossipy hour and I think it helped girls when they got to senior school.'

Christmas

Christmas was always magical. The front hall was decorated and a rope of laurel leaves fixed round the walls. An illuminated crib was put in the arch beneath the stairs of the inner hall. There were musical plays, children's parties in the drawing room, and a party for the whole school with entertainers. There was a noisy Christmas tea during which Father Christmas, (the husband of one of the staff members) arrived. Great ingenuity was displayed in his method of arrival. 'Once a boot was seen descending from above through the hall window. On another occasion, bells were heard and antlers appeared outside the dining room window.' Miss Burke made miniature toy animals in costume as Christmas gifts for each boarder. Staff were not forgotten either – every member was given a gift and a personal, cryptic poem. The girls gave members of staff a present, too, accompanied by a short verse and staff would have to guess to whom it referred. The party ended with everyone singing *The Holly and the Ivy*. Then, watched by the visitors, Miss Burke led a crocodile of staff and children round the rooms, up to the dormitories and down again into the hall, where the unbroken chain wound into a spiral with Miss Burke at the centre, until everyone was back down. On another night, the boarders in their dressing gowns came into the front hall and the stairs to sing and listen to carols. Dr Hall, one of the governors, and his group appeared, dressed in Victorian garb, ringing handbells.

School customs

When the school day ended, day pupils went into the covered way and shook hands, always wearing their white cotton gloves, and bobbed a curtsy to Miss Burke or another member of staff. At the end of term, all the staff lined up to shake hands with every child, which gave the staff an opportunity to bid farewell to the school leavers.

On the last night of the Summer Term, the leavers buried their church pennies under the sundial on the front lawn. On one occasion, two of them got locked out and spent the early hours shivering in the drawing room conservatory!

Miss Burke leaves

In 1978, Miss Burke's mother died. Her father needed care but refused to live at the school. So, after 20 years at MG, at the peak of her career, Miss Burke reluctantly resigned as Headmistress and left the teaching profession to look after her father.

CHAPTER FIVE

MRS
ASPREY'S
ERA
1978–1988

The Lapraik Hall

THE LAPRAIK WING

His name was also given to The Lapraik Hall, the new gym. While this was being built in 1985, a pair of mistlethrushes were building their nest in the angle of one of the girders. In typical British fashion, building work on this corner was put in abeyance until the eggs had hatched and the fledglings had flown the nest.

After Paula Burke left at the end of the Autumn Term 1977, there was a hiatus. Barbara Asprey, appointed as the new Headmistress, was unable to start until the Summer Term of 1978. Mrs Molly Reddington, one of the teachers, stood in as acting Head for the Spring term and came to live at the school with her husband, Douglas.

Barbara Asprey had previously taught at MG for six years, in charge of Group II, a lively class

The Lapraik Wing, opened in 1981

of 6 year olds. She then became Deputy Head and was responsible for putting part-time teaching staff on to the national Burnham Scale of salaries, so that they were on a par with full-time staff already on that scale. She left the school for a period to become the Headmistress of The Vicarage School in Richmond, before returning to MG as its Headmistress.

In the early years of Mrs Asprey's headship, the school acquired the freehold of the grounds and buildings, which was a prerequisite of MG acquiring charitable status. It was then that new building plans went ahead. In 1981 the old glasshouse pottery building and the old coach house, which had been adapted for use as an art room, were both demolished. Both had deteriorated badly and the art room roof leaked. During the demolition, the builder discovered two signatures on some wooden cladding, one was that of an apprentice, and the segment of wood was presented to the school.

The new block comprised an art room and two further classrooms. It was named *The Lapraik Wing* after the current Chairman, Col. Ian Lapraik, a wartime hero. His name was also given to *The Lapraik Hall*, the new gym. While this was being built in 1985, a pair of mistlethrushes were building their nest in the angle of one of the girders. In typical British fashion, building work on this corner was put in abeyance until the eggs had hatched and the fledglings had flown the nest.

Two pupils, Melanie Dean and Claire Bagehot wrote a piece about this, entitled *The First Inhabitants of the New Hall.* 'The mistlethrush, the biggest of all the thrushes, seemed completely undisturbed by all the commotion surrounding her, and the workmen built round the nest. When she had completed her nest she laid four light-blue speckled eggs. After approximately a fortnight, three eggs hatched. The babies were covered in down and were as greedy as they were cute. The parents then had a hard task of finding enough food for the chicks and themselves. While we were watching them from the common room window, one parent returned with a worm every five minutes or so. After nearly two weeks, one daring baby bird managed to flap his wings hard enough to rise up several inches. The other two birds are now starting to stretch their wings ready to fly and we hope by next week they will be gone, because they are holding up part of the work.'

There were also two new laboratories, a further classroom, a new music block with practice rooms, a common room and quarters for resident staff. On the sports side, there were three new hard tennis courts, two hard netball courts an athletics track and a hockey field.

As the school expanded in numbers, Mrs Asprey divided the school into six Houses, rather than four. Instead of male heroes, each House was named after a famous woman – *Nightingale, Curie, Cavell, Pankhurst, Aylward* and *Thatcher.*

The science laboratories (1976 – 1990)

Science

Maltman's Green was one of the first girls' preparatory schools to provide first-class facilities
for science. The purpose-built science laboratory in the new classroom block in 1976 served the
school well for 14 years. Wendy Wilson, Head of Science from 1974 to 1997, was responsible
both for the development of the subject in the school and for the design and development of a
brand-new science block, which included a junior laboratory, a senior laboratory and a computer
room. She said, 'They are considerably superior to any of the boys' prep school laboratories I saw
when I went to IAPS science meetings every year. I couldn't help noticing when I attended these
meetings in the 1980s and 1990s, that the elderly prep schoolmasters tended to think that only
boys did proper science and that girls only dabbled in a little nature study! One of them wrote
a textbook in which all the illustrations showed only boys doing experiments. I complained
to Longmans, the publishers, who ate humble pie and revised subsequent editions.'

Over the years, science became a more important part of the school curriculum. In the
Common Entrance exams, a compulsory science paper was introduced at 11+, to add to the
papers at 12+ and 13+. Science lessons increased from two a week in 1974 to five or six sessions

a week by the 1980s. Electronics and computers were introduced. Wendy Wilson continually updated her skills by attending courses, and two more science teachers were appointed. Wendy Wilson retired in 2000 after twenty five years at the school. She had placed great importance on practical laboratory skills and safety issues, saying, 'I was pleased that during all my years at Maltman's Green, no child ever had an accident in the science laboratories.'

Art

Pauline Hodder was the Head of Art from 1968 until 1990. She was not sympathetic when parents told her, 'There is no one artistic in my family', or when girls told her they couldn't draw. Her message to parents and girls was 'You can learn art, as you learn to play the piano, swim, write, and do maths. Drawing talent is *not* a necessity but a bonus!'

Art had always been a specialist subject and Craft, Design, Technology (CDT), the new subject introduced in senior schools, had been already anticipated by her in a simplified form at MG, 'to lay the foundation of aesthetic judgements and creative ability, and to stimulate an awareness of an interest in design together with an appreciation of the Fine Arts.' *Art, Craft and Design* became her new title for this subject.

The unpopular, time-consuming chore for the art teacher at the end of each term was sticking the pupils' report pictures on to each report. Barbara Asprey passed this job to the Group teachers, and, needless to say, it was not popular with them either. The school was fast becoming too big for this type of report format, which had to be completed by the teachers at school. The format was changed instead to a folder containing a page for each subject, which could be written up by staff at home.

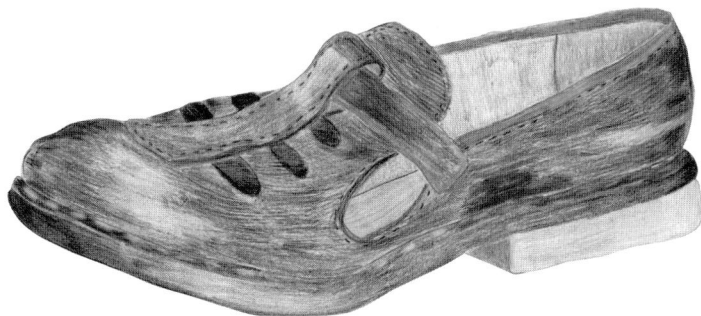

Two drawings done in Miss Hodder's art classes

The art room in 1981

One aspect of art in which Pauline Hodder excelled was designing the major costumes and theatrical scenery for the school's musical/dramatic productions every Christmas. She was particularly remembered for Cinderella's coach and her crocodile and cuckoo costumes. She also designed the layout of several of MG's annual school magazines. But her most enduring design is the Maltman's Green school logo, still used today. This came about almost by accident. While penning the yearly Roll of Honour of pupils' names, there was a space left – and the logo was devised to fit the space.

In 1985, Miss Hodder was joined by an assistant, Ronnie Powell, who later succeeded her, and they split art teaching between them. At Christmas time, for example, Ronnie Powell took over the responsibility for the decorations of the hall. Teaching pottery had ceased for a time after the original pottery was demolished and Nora Kay had left. Eventually, a small room was made into a pottery and a kiln was installed elsewhere. Pottery began again and became part of the art curriculum under Ronnie Powell.

Music

The high standards set by Miss Holland in Miss Chambers' and Miss Burke's time still continued, both for instrumentalists and choral work. Shirley Massey, fired by Miss Burke's enthusiasm for musical plays, not only composed the music but wrote her own libretti for a yearly series of musical entertainments. *What's New?* was based on the mistlethrush episode in the building of *Lapraik Hall*. Other mini-operettas included

Miss Hodder's crocodile costume

The Snow Queen, Once upon a Time, Everybody's Darlings and a repeat performance of *We're all going to Bethlehem*. Shirley Massey wrote, 'It never ceased to amaze me that our little girls could have so much talent and could rise to the occasion with heaps of confidence and aplomb. There was always just the right person waiting in the wings to slot into the part – singers, dancers, actors and musicians all through the school. The sung choruses were an integral part of each show.'

Mrs Asprey was very keen to have a school orchestra and various instruments were donated and bought. Music was taught at all levels twice a week and girls learned a diverse range of instruments from visiting instrumentalists – not only piano, but also cello, flute, oboe,

The cast of the Snow Queen

clarinet, guitar, bassoon and saxophone and, at a later stage, percussion. This proved yet another problem for timetabling. Lunch hours now became occupied with choir practice, orchestra playing and the recorder ensemble.

Physical Education

When the new *Lapraik Hall* was completed and fully equipped for gymnastics and games, Miss Journet was able to develop PE to the full. 'We now had a perfect full-sized floor area and all the equipment necessary for Olympic style gymnastics. Both the children and I revelled in the choreography and the floor work – individual and group. I soon discovered that the interest and expertise were incredible. So many talented girls with such enthusiasm, courage and dedication.

'They were heady days for Maltman's Green. We travelled hundreds of miles in *Gully* (the school bus) with the Under-11 and Under-13 teams to attend championships in many parts of England. Without exception we were always among the Individual and Team winners, more often than not holding the Gold.'

Pat Journet and her teams became so well-known that she was invited to attend a meeting with the head of the PE Department at Millfield. They planned a format for the IAPS Gymnastics Championships which holds to this day. By now every possible sport in the curriculum was practised, even table tennis and yoga for the seniors. A number of girls went on to make PE their career.

The school and parents

Parents had always been greatly involved in the activities of the school since Miss Burke's time, and had been especially helpful preparing costumes and scenery for dramatic productions and setting up stalls for the school's summer fairs. Soon after Mrs Asprey became Head, she wanted to put parental involvement on to a more formal footing, by setting up a *Parents' Society*.
A number of the parents were already interested and a meeting of parents was held in May 1979, when a committee was formed under the Chairmanship of Mrs Comino-James. As well as the committee officers, there was a representative for each class year and one for the staff. The agreed aims were 'to promote good relations between all parents and staff, and to encourage a friendly atmosphere throughout the school on all levels.' The *Friends of Maltman's Green* also helped to supply equipment for the new gym, computer room, library and music department, as well as installing an adventure playground.

Mrs Asprey retired in 1988 to Henley, to look after her husband, who had become ill.

CHAPTER SIX

MRS
EVANS'
ERA
1988–1998

'SO VERY MALTMAN'S GREEN'

'Let your daughter dream her own dreams and not yours. Then, if those dreams do not come true, she may be disappointed, but at least she will not feel guilty.'

Of all the Headmistresses in the years since Miss Chambers' era, Mrs Evans comes closest to expounding and putting into practice Miss Chambers' philosophy. To the golden-oldie pupils from the pre-1945 years, this would seem surprising, given that Mrs Evans had come from Roedean – 'known as a schooly school.' Mrs Evans' first position after leaving university was at Roedean, the well-known girls' Public School, and then several years later she became the Head of Junior House, a separate House at Roedean for girls from 9 to 13. She held this post with distinction for three years before being appointed Headmistress of Maltman's Green.

From the outset, at her interview in Ma's beautiful unchanged drawing room, Mrs Evans felt the magic of Maltman's Green, its ethos and its character. 'Headmistresses come and Headmistresses go, and we meet the challenges in our day in our individual ways. For a while something of us is reflected in the school. But Maltman's Green is a very special place and it has a life of its own, which is somehow constant in the face of change.'

When Madeleine Evans came to MG in 1988, with her Cavalier spaniel in attendance, she knew that she had inherited a strong school with excellence in the arts, in science, music and PE, and she wanted it to continue as a strong school despite the different social, economic and educational challenges. She believed in the value of academic education, but saw education as primarily about social values, personal awareness, and development of potential in mind, body and spirit. Speaking to a meeting of parents at a Friends of Maltman's Green AGM, she echoed Ma's sentiments when she said, 'My aim is for every child to discover a talent while she is at MG. Will your child discover a talent for a particular subject, not necessarily an academic one? Did you know that she had perfect pitch, a flair for design, the suppleness and control to do a backward somersault? Has your daughter discovered a talent for friendship? What a joy to herself and others that will be. A talent for seeing the other person's point of view? A talent for compromise? A talent for leadership? A talent for working as part of a team? I cannot over-stress the importance for the future of co-operative work skills.'

She wanted to encourage the potential of the young girls in her charge. 'I want us to be good at encouraging achievement and I want us to do this with kindness and sensitivity to the different levels of potential in the individual.'

One of the problems she had encountered with young pupils was their worries about not coming up to their parents' expectations. They wanted the approval of their parents, and had worked hard, but had not necessarily gained the grades in examinations which they knew their parents had hoped for. They had done their best and came tearfully to Mrs Evans to ask her to mediate with their parents. In speaking to parents, Mrs Evans, like Ma, told them they should compare their daughter's progress with her own past prowess, not with the achievements of other girls. 'Let your daughter dream her own dreams and not yours. Then, if those dreams do not come true, she may be disappointed, but at least she will not feel guilty.

'Confidence must come first. Therefore, in the early years, we do our best to avoid competition that might destroy confidence. We encourage the girls to compete against their own past achievements and set them individual and attainable goals. We know from experience that the pecking order, published too early, can become a stifling, self-fulfilling prophecy, which does not stimulate anyone in the pile. The idea of marks is only introduced gradually. How many children who came second and are justly proud of their achievements are deflated by the thoughtless, "Well done, but who came first?" When confidence is less fragile, the exposure to competition, especially competition between groups, plays a useful part. It celebrates success but takes the edge off losing by making it less personal.'

However, she believed in competition because it is a fact of life. 'We do our children a grave disservice if we do not prepare them for it. We, as adults, know that we cannot all be first and perhaps the true success lies in how we cope with our failures. Resilience is life-saving.'

Her belief in discipline and rules was different from that of Ma's, because she was dealing with a younger age group. She saw rules as necessary to provide a structure for civilised living. 'Children generally like the security of rules and they are happy when they have clear guidelines as to what is expected of them. Knowing when to turn a blind eye in the interest of compassion is important too.' She saw discipline as consideration for others. 'I want the children to look me in the eye and smile when they make way for me around the school. I do not want them to try to disappear into the walls in terror.'

This is illustrated by her attitude, very reminiscent of Ma's, to a misdemeanour on the part of the senior boarders. On the last day of a summer term, the voluminous bra belonging to Matron was found flying on the school flagpole! Mrs Evans was disarmed when the girls said, 'It was quite all right and no one had been put in danger', because their most competent gymnast, with a superior sense of balance, had elected to go on the roof, knowing it would be safe for her.

Her girls also put the good of others first. On one occasion, when the woodwind ensemble

Crystal Downing *(left)*, **winner of a music scholarship to Roedean, in 1994**

was about to play for parents, one of the key players could not find her instrument. She looked high and low but, as it could not be found, was resigned to cancelling her performance. Without any prompting, another member of the ensemble gave up her instrument, thus forfeiting her own opportunity to perform. She said, 'It was the only thing to do.'

Like Ma, Mrs Evans employed teachers with their feet on the ground, who had a sense of humanity and a good sense of humour. 'A good teacher needs to make use of any or all the techniques at her disposal according to the needs of her pupils.' Following a broad-based curriculum, girls were encouraged to reach a good standard in all subjects, as well as the arts and sports. For instance, in 1988, a girl gained a major art scholarship to Roedean and, in 1993, girls gained two academic scholarships to Benenden, a music scholarship to Cheltenham Ladies' College and a sports bursary to Millfield.

To help parents with their choice of a senior school, Mrs Evans organised a mini-education exhibition with thirty major schools taking part. 'At a time when we are bombarded with league tables, which are meaningless because they tell us grades achieved not potential fulfilled, we must remind ourselves that the best school is only best if it brings out the best in our child.'

One of the recent developments in the National Curriculum wove several strands into Personal, Social and Health Education (PSHE). It covered everything at the appropriate times from basic hygiene, such as washing your hands before eating, to sensible eating, drugs and sex education. At MG this teaching started in the nursery years, and was reinforced in assemblies.

In 1995, after a two day OFSTED registration visit, the school received a favourable report. 'Standards are good in all subjects visited. Pupils read and write well and their spelling is good. Their knowledge and understanding is sound. They are hard-working and articulate in discussion. Teaching is well-planned and carefully executed with a good working atmosphere in lessons.' They also extolled the virtues of MG's spacious grounds, seen as a great asset to the school.

New buildings

Each year, there was new development with new buildings. The original house was still seen as the heart of the school and remained unaltered, and new buildings were constructed in a style that blended in, to give a feel of continuity and settled confidence. The new classroom buildings were grouped round a central, hard-surface playground and linked by cloister-like covered ways, that echoed the style of the old house. In this period, the new classroom block had specialist teaching rooms, including a language laboratory; a science wing with two laboratories, one of which was designated for design technology, and an IT centre. A new kindergarten was also built to accommodate a three-form entry.

Boarding

In 1994, a courageous decision was made to phase out boarding. The recession hit several groups of parents, who might traditionally have chosen boarding schools for their children. For example,

The Science and Technology Block, opened in 1990

allowances for boarding places for children living abroad were much reduced in many multi-national companies, the armed forces and diplomatic services. These places were not taken up by potential boarders in Great Britain because, here too, the recession had bitten. Moreover, many parents had become more involved in the education of their children and now preferred to send their girls to day schools. Madeleine Evans emphasised that though the structure of the school was changing, 'the commitment to a child's all-round education and well-being that lies at the heart of boarding, will remain.'

Instead, Maltman's Green offered an extended day to children who needed it. Pupils could be dropped off at the school between 7.30 and 8.30am, to be supervised and to enjoy a sociable breakfast. At the end of the day, the older girls could do their prep at school, while the younger ones could enjoy play activities until they were picked up by their parents. In the Summer Term, prospective school leavers to boarding schools were able to enjoy a week of boarding to acclimatize themselves to this new experience.

An invitation and programme covers for musical events

Music and musical events

The Christmas musicals continued to be enjoyed with new works written by Shirley Massey – *The Wonders of Alice, The Magic Fishbone* and *The Christmas Cuckoo,* and earlier musicals were given a further hearing.

By the end of the Summer Term, many girls reached a very high standard of performance and played some quite demanding music at the summer concerts. The school was very proud of Crystal Downing, a pianist and flautist, who won a music scholarship to Roedean in 1994.

Several girls attended the Wellington College weekend preparatory school orchestral courses and IAPS choral courses. The senior choir enjoyed singing with other choirs at Eton College Chapel under the auspices of the Royal Schools of Church Music. This special service for schools was entitled *Angels Unaware.*

Regular pleasurable visits were made on Saturday mornings to the Ernest Read Association concerts for schools, held in the Royal Festival Hall in London. Special highlights were the opera matinée performances for schools at the Royal Opera House, Covent Garden. These operas included *Tosca, The Tales of Hoffman, A Masked Ball,* and *Carmen.*

Friends of Maltman's Green (FOMG)

The Friends organisation, started in Miss Asprey's time, had gone from strength to strength. In 1993, Mrs Evans spoke at their AGM, saying, 'The Friends of Maltman's Green, with their gift of playground equipment, that can be enjoyed by the whole school, have acknowledged the importance of play to children. Play is also important to adults and so my thanks go to Mrs Stone for her spirited leadership, and to the committee for working so hard to provide a series of social events where adults have played too!'

Other funding projects put the gilt on the gingerbread. The Friends' Computer Fund enabled the school to install a system in the IT room, and later funded a project to identify and protect the flora and fauna found in the spacious grounds of the school.

Mrs Evans had a great rapport with the Friends' organisation and, at a surprise barbecue party held to mark her farewell, said, 'It may be a contradiction, coming from someone who has been conspicuously building and re-equipping for years, but the unparalleled facilities that the girls enjoy are not what I care about most. It's the people who use them who matter to me … Today you have given me a lovely party … but your ultimate gift to me has been allowing me to play a part in your daughters' lives. Maltman's Green girls are my stake in the future too.'

Independent Schools Council Annual Digest, 2002

After Mrs Evans left, the first ever annual digest of inspection reports on schools within the Independent Schools Council (ISC) was published in 2002, prepared by Tony Hubbard, Director of ISC. The problem he posed in the digest was that the combination of public examinations with league tables and the intensive preparation for tests and examinations often amounted to spoon-feeding. He felt that teachers and schools had a real dilemma because, 'spoon-feeding works, but it works at the risk of something British schools have always been good at: turning out young people to be inventive, creative, independent minded, even awkward'. He continued, 'Spoon-feeding works because examination and its marking, carefully moderated and published to be fair and predictable, can be reduced to a formula. However, the economic, political and social world for which pupils are being prepared today is characterised not by predictability, but by its opposite – uncertainty, unpredictability – and the need to be able to make rational decisions based on incomplete information or, in fact, conflicting attitudes and opinions.' This endorses Mrs Evans' statement that 'the great challenge in education today is to fit children for a future that we can only guess at. All we can say for sure is that it will be different from the past, and will require a flexibility of skills and attitudes that most of us were not taught at school.'

Mrs Evans went on to say, 'The willingness to do something for the good of the team is not an outmoded 1930s' virtue that should have gone out with gym slips and lisle stockings, it is essential for success in the 21st century. I firmly believe that in the future the great advances in every field from research to consumption will be team-based …my immediate concern is to give the girls the basic enthusiasms and techniques for co-operative work.'

The wheel has come full circle. Many of Miss Chambers' original ideas underline both Madeleine Evans' and the ISI pronouncements. Ma abhorred 'spoon-feeding' and her ideas about project work, self-expression, fulfilling a child's potential, confidence, resourcefulness, initiative and the importance of extra-curricular activities are vindicated. Pamela Neal Green, an MG girl from the 1930s, saw her contemporaries as having a 'tackle anything' quality about them. This is the very quality which is needed in our uncertain world of today.

CHAPTER SEVEN

MALTMAN'S GREEN
TODAY

MALTMAN'S GREEN TODAY

'The pupils are valued as individuals and we want each girl to discover and develop her own talents and strengths, and be prepared to meet the challenge of the modern world.'

Today, Maltman's Green is a large, thriving non-denominational girls' preparatory day school providing nursery and primary places for girls from the age of 3 to 11. Currently the school has around 380 girls on its roll. They are taught in 25 classes, which never have more than 20 children, and often fewer. Admission to the school is usually at the age of 3+ into the nursery or at 4 into the kindergarten.

The nursery entrants are admitted by order of registration, although siblings of children already at the school are given priority. Pupils applying for entry after kindergarten are assessed by taking the National Foundation of Education Research (NFER) standardised tests, which enable the school to be selective should it wish. However, all classes in the early years are mixed-ability and the school does not cater only for able pupils. In 2000, 5% of the girls came from families where English is not their first language and about 20 girls were identified as requiring special educational provision.

A recent Maltman's Green brochure states: 'The pupils are valued as individuals and we want each girl to discover and develop her own talents and strengths, and be prepared to meet the challenge of the modern world. As well as achieving high educational standards and the successful transfer of pupils at 11 to a wide range of senior schools, Maltman's Green aims to foster personal qualities such as self-reliance, determination, confidence and respect for others.'

Miss Julia Reynolds, the Headmistress, sees diversity and the richness of the school's programme as key factors for parental choice of Maltman's Green for their girls. But more importantly 'the girls are encouraged to aim high and face life's challenges philosophically and with enthusiasm. To give of one's best, and not to crumple at the first hurdle, is paramount.'

The school aims to provide high academic standards and to serve the needs of all of its girls and the wider community by providing a broad education which will give a firm foundation for the next stage of the educational ladder. The school prepares the girls to move to both maintained schools such as Buckinghamshire grammar schools, and to independent schools. Pupils continue to be accepted into their first choice of school at the age of 11, many of them gaining scholarships.

Independent Schools Inspectorate (ISI)

The school governors, the Headmistress and all the teaching staff had reason to feel proud of the report on Maltman's Green by the ISI in 2000. The overall summary 'is that Maltman's Green is a very good school. The Headmistress has a clear vision for the school and provides strong, dynamic leadership. The standards are high and the girls make significant progress as they move through the school. The teaching and commitment of all the staff are strengths of the school. Pastoral care and concern for the welfare of pupils is very good and the girls are looked after in a caring, loving way. The pupils benefit from a wide range of extra-curricular activities.'

Physical Education

The school's reputation in sporting activities is exceptionally high and sports play a very big part in life of the school. In gymnastics, Maltman's Green has been the IAPS National Champion for

The school's gymnasts have been IAPS National Champions for four years running

A netball game in 2003

four years running, and second in the country in the IAPS Netball National Championships. Every pupil has a PE lesson every day. Miss Reynolds believes 'that good physical health and fitness and the highest level of intellectual attainment are inextricably linked. But she also sees sport as offering 'opportunities for girls to shine when they might otherwise not do so on the academic front.' Girls learn that the team effort is crucial, and that learning to work together and to share is one of the most valuable lessons in life.

The Arts

Art, music and drama play a big part in school activities. All girls have the opportunity to take part in a dramatic production in the course of the year. Recent mini West End productions, enabling the girls to work collaboratively, have included *The Mikado, Little Shop of Horrors, The Pied Piper, The Pirates of Penzance* – enjoyed by performers and audience alike.

The time capsule – a link with the past

In 2002 to celebrate the Queen's Golden Jubilee, Maltman's Green buried a time capsule beneath some commemorative trees in the walled garden. It contained an assortment of memorabilia relating to the school today, as it was at the time of the Queen's Coronation and as it was in Miss Chamber's era.

Focussing on the past was a fascinating experience for the preparatory school children. When they discussed the early years of MG, they were amused, intrigued, shocked and envious in turn. Shocked and amused at sloshing in stable yard at the height of summer (which one old girl said 'would not be allowed today!') and the uniform akin to boy's clothes worn by Ma's younger pupils. Envious of the freedom to sleep out under the stars, the free time given to girls to pursue their own interests, and the lack of rules in Ma's time, which they understood related to much older girls.

However, Ma's ethos 'to enable children to be themselves,' has filtered down through the years. Today's pupils are encouraged to develop self expression and given the opportunity to be enterprising, and through their many experiences, continue to make the world around them a richer place.

Burying the time capsule

Music – the golden thread

The strong musical tradition continues, with many girls playing instruments, so that they can take part in the orchestra, the string group, jazz band, flute group, wind band and recorder groups, as well as singing in the choir. Music has been the golden thread running through Maltman's Green – from Miss Holland's music lessons to talented girls at 6d a minute in the 1920s; her choral excellence with memorable carols, including *When Christ was Born* by Reineke, so cherished by girls in the 1930s and 1940s; through to *We're all going to Bethlehem* in Miss Burke's time; Shirley Massey's yearly musical entertainments in the 1970s and 1980s, including *What's New?* based on the mistlethrushes in *Lapraik Hall*; the MG choir taking part in *Angels Unaware* at Eton College Chapel in the 1990s; and finally, MG's musical apotheosis in 2003, when the school won the Junior *Songs of Praise* School Choir of the Year, in the first BBC *Celebrate* competition for Senior and Junior schools. To enter, Maltman's Green submitted tapes of their choir's performance. The best entries went into the second round, when BBC producers visited the schools, held workshops and gave musical advice on the hymns. The short-listed contestants took part in a concert at Symphony Hall, Birmingham, and MG was chosen from six finalists as the winner of the Junior Schools. Not only the present staff, parents and pupils took pride in the choir's performance but many old girls and staff, who watched the choir on TV, rejoiced to hear and see the confidence, competence, and the obvious enjoyment of the girls, in working together to put on a good show that was 'so very Maltman's Green.'

The winning choir

APPENDIX

GIRLS IN THE 1920S

Renee Ascherson, Betty Barrow, T. Barlow, B. Balfour, M. Baxter, Rachel Benton-Jones, Enid Berridge, Cynthia Burnley, Grizel Blackwood Murray, Dorothy Collingham, Mary Crabtree, N. Crowther, Jo Curzon, Giva Dane, Nancy Davies, Evelyn Dodd, Diana Escourt, P. Falconer, Joyce Fitch, Rosalind Fitch, L. Frost, M. Fury, E. Gatti, V. Grantham, Billie Guthe, Maxine Harding, L. Hiscox, S. Hoesgood, E. Holland, D. Howarth, Bubbles Lemon, L. Levene, Angelica Lloyd, Ursula Lord, M. McTurk, E. MacCowan, A. Miller, Joan Montefiore, N. Nixon, Alison Nugent, C. Paget, F. Priest, J. Ritzema, N. Ritzema, Elizabeth Robinson, Katharine Robinson (Kato), Helen Robinson, Marian Robinson, J. Roper, Pam Roper, Nancy Russell-Davies, Esther Salaman, Jill Salaman, Susan Salaman, Betty Sale, W. Scarf, Jean Scarth, R. Shaw, L. Slater, Audrey Saunders, May Scott, E. Stevenson, K. Stott, May Verity, Johnny Walker, Cynthia Walter, Mamie Watson, Sheila Wenham, Pam Woodhead.

GIRLS IN THE 1930S AND 1940S

Moira Albery, Mary Behrens, Ruth Behrens (Boo), Jo Bembaron, Joyce Bennett, Rachel Benton-Jones, June Best, Anne Blackett, Elizabeth Blackett (Wizz), Betty Broadhead, Lavender Bruce, Alison Burnley, Molly Burton, Joy Catchpole, Joan Chadwick, Suzanne Chambers, Barbara Chippindall (Chippy), Valerie Corcas, Peggy Cripps, Theresa Cripps (Cheesy), Maureen Currie, Joyce Cutbush, Helen Danby, Donna D'Arcy Clark, Lizzie Davidson, Honor Davy, Ursula Davy, Hazel Dodds, Jo Dodds, Rhona Dowson, Shirra Duff, Elspeth Duxbury, Ann Early, Caty Early, Eleanor Early (Oll), Freddie Eisler, Pam Ells, Heather English, Diana Faunthorpe, Moyca Field, Molly Fitch, Carol Foster, Eileen Fothergill, Monica Foucard, Joan Furnival, Muriel Garstang, Nancy Gilliatt, Celia Gold, Diana Gollancz, Margaret Gunning (Muggin), Anne Haigh, Gisele Haiman, Annette Hambly, Lois Hambly, Pauline Hambly, Phyllis Hankey, Maxine Harding, Grizelda Heaton-Armstrong, Audrey Hinchliffe, Barbara Harper, Jean Harper, Jane Howson, Mary Howson, Clare Hunter, Annette Ingold, Margaret Jackson, Anne Johnstone, Michelle Jones (Mickey), Margaret Keesey, Helen Knowles, Angelica Lloyd, Bridgit Luard, Jean Mackellar, Margaret Mackellar, Doris McBride, Barbara McMurray, Dorothea McMurray (Dorrie), Margaret McMurray (Peggy), Rosalind Mellowes, Lois Mitchinson, Averil Byers, Averil Moir, Jean Mary Montague, Cynthia Morris, Valerie Morris, Hazel Murray, Joyce Murray, Lesley Neal Green, Pamela Neal Green, Peggy Neal Green, Sheila Neal Green, Jane Noel, Anne Overton, Jean Priest,

GIRLS IN THE 1930S AND 1940S (continued)

Mary Priest, Barbara Priestley, Sylvia Priestley, Jennifer Ramage, Mildred Rawson, Anne Robinson, Elspeth Robinson, Betty Sale (Snails), Pam Sale, Marcia Sandberg, Diana Sanderson (Dinkles), Susan Sanderson, Jean Scarth, Olive Scott, Margaret Shaw, Irene Simmons, Meg Simmons, Betty Staib, Jane Ann Sterndale Bennett, Marguerite Sutherland (Miggy), Anne Sutherland (Bungy), Mary Temple Thurston, Anne Todd, Elizabeth Todd, Janet Tombs, Anne Trimmer, Diana Tywritt-Drake, Joan Tywritt-Drake, Jill Van Duzer, Pat Van Duzer, Barbara Woodhead, Betty Woodhead, Phyllis Wiley, Pam Wildman, Hersey Williamson, Sylvia Winter.

STAFF IN THE 1930S AND 1940S

Miss Armstrong, Mr Arrowsmith, Miss Baron (Barry), Miss Barker, Mlle. Bauer, Miss Enid Berridge, Miss Bird, Miss Cook (Chef), Miss Cummuski, Mrs Daley, Miss Nancy Davies, Miss Fanchiotti (Fan), Miss Rose Hamilton, Miss Tibbie Hardie, Miss Pip Hardwick, Miss Lyn Hardy, Frl. Hayman, Miss Hemans, Miss Margaret Hirst (Hirstie), Miss Hodgkiss, Miss Holland (Rah), Miss Molly Kemp (Kempie), Miss Lindsay, Miss McCulloch, Miss Nan Mitchell, Miss Newton (Frailty), Miss Margaret Parry, Miss Pearson, Miss Helen Robinson, Mlle. Ronsin, Miss Nancy Russell-Davies, Mlle. Schaugren, Frl. Seuffert, Miss Selby, Frl. von Simson, Miss Strombom, Miss Taylor, Miss Rosemary Topping, Mlle. Verchere, Miss Molly Warr, Miss Mamie Watson, Miss Sheila Wenham, Miss Barbara Wimperis, Miss West, Miss Nina Woodcock

GIRLS IN 1949

Hazel Adeley, Monica Angelasto, Shirley Barnes, Sylvia (Dickie) Bird, Mary Bridgen, Anne Byam Shaw, Juliet Byam Shaw, Janet Cameron, Doreen Cashman, Joanna Cook, Rosemary Cornwall-Leigh, Caroline Crutwell, Jane Crutwell, Shaney Davis, Mary Elliot, Alison Ewen, Maggy Ewen, Anne-Marie Fenton, Shirley France, Jane Francis, Jean Fryer, Tammy Fuerst, Zara Gabbe, Celia Gold, Geraldine Gosling, Susan Hadland, Betty Hadley-Jones, Zan Harris, Lorline Higgan, Betty Hoppit, Julia House, Barbara Jacob, Jane Jacobs, Elizabeth James, Rosalind Lamin, Dutchy van Lennop, Colleen Luttrell, Mary Macaskie, Alison Middlebrook, Virginia Mills, Shirley Moore, Jane Page, Jane Proctor, Sarah Proctor, Mary Riley, Belinda Scott, Jane Scott, -- Scott, Norma Scott-Wood, Toni Simons, Helen Simpson (Twinkle), Jill Simpson, Susan Smith, Trixie Smith, Katia Stoddart, Dansey Sorley, Elizabeth Stanner, Meryl Thomas, Sally Twist, Paula Wheatley-Dyson, Alicia Watson, Susan Whitfield, Deborah Wigham, Merle Williams, Ursula Williams, Cecily --, Hilary - , Janice --, Jenny--, June --, Kim --, Susan --.

STAFF IN 1949

Miss Arrowsmith, Miss Bruce, Mrs Chalmers, Miss Echalaz, Miss Egles, Miss Good, Matron Griffiths, Miss Haley, Miss Hinchey (Nelly), Miss Holland, - - Leary, Mrs Parish, Miss Rowe, Esther Salaman, Miss Tucker (Tommy), Mrs Vincent, Miss Withers

STAFF 1974-2000

(from a compilation by Mrs Wendy Wilson)

HEADS OF DEPARTMENTS

Art Pauline Hodder, Ronnie Powell

English Diane Carolyn, Rosemary Hales

French Pat Buchanan, Marie-Noelle Stacey

Geography Vicki Russell

IT Valerie Till

Maths Jackie Calow

Music Veronica Bennetts, Hilary Mason, Shirley Massey

PE Beverley Humphreys, Pat Journet

RE Val Welford

Science Hazel Collins, Wendy Wilson

Head of Junior School

Sue Jupp

TEACHING STAFF – OVER 3 YEARS SERVICE

Kate Bennett, Julie Bennetts, Jenni Blunt, Jenny Bolt, Frances Borer, Carolyn Boyle, Zara Cairns, Shirley Clarke, Wendy Cook, Barbara Crawford, Christine Davies, Maureen Davies, Jo Dewhurst, Shan Harvey, Mary Hembrow, Margaret Hylton, Ros Johnstone, Margaret Kirshner, Nicolette Lethbridge, Christine Lever, Kay Lovejoy, Margaret Mace, Sheila Murley, Cynthia Patterson, Pauline Smith, Mary Stretton, Evelyn Turnhill, Molly Voyce, Kathleen White, Ann Wood-Smith, Caroline Yollands

REFERENCES

FOREWORD

Report of the Consultative Committee on the Primary School (The Hadow Report). (HMSO, London, 1931)

Central Advisory Council for Education (England), *Children and their Primary Schools. (The Plowden Report).* (HMSO, London, 1967)

Berry Mayall, *Sociologies of Childhood and Educational Thinking.* (Institute of Education, London, 2003)

CHAPTER 1   HISTORY OF THE BUILDING AND THE GROUNDS

Jennie Fletcher, *History of the Building.* Research from the Head Office of the Society of Friends in London, Jordans Friends Meeting House and the Parish Church of Chalfont St. Peter. (Unpublished MSS)

Algernon Drummond, *Memories of Maltman's Green.* (Unpublished MSS, 1971)

CHAPTER 2   MISS CHAMBERS' ERA

Trevor Blewitt, ed., *The Modern Schools Handbook.* (Camelot Press, 1934)

   Chapter: Beatrice E. Chambers, *Maltman's Green School.*

Ruth J Pilkington, *Memories of Maltman's Green1934–1941.* (Unpublished MSS)

Cynthia Walton, *Boarding School. (*Unpublished MSS)

Caty Crawford, Lady Flowers, ed., *Maltman's Green Reunion Booklet.*

  The Beginning

Trevor Blewitt, ed., *The Modern Schools Handbook.* Editor's Foreword and Introduction for Parents by Annabel Williams-Ellis. (op.cit.)

  Choosing Maltman's Green

The New Statesman and Nation, *Advertisement for Maltman's Green.* (July 3, 1937)

  War and the end of an era

Diary of Audrey Priestman. (Unpublished MSS)

CHAPTER 3   MISS LOWE'S ERA

Nora Kay, *The Greenhouse Effect.* (CPA News, No. 5, May/June, 1989)

CHAPTER 4   MISS BURKE'S ERA

Maltman's Green in crisis

Maltman's Green Parents' Association. (January 28,1963)

Buckinghamshire Advertiser, *School Closure Bid.* (October 3, 1963)

Buckinghamshire Advertiser, *School Take-over Battle.* (October 24, 1963)

Buckinghamshire Advertiser, *Parents Plan to Take Over Girls' School.* (November 22, 1963)

Buckinghamshire Advertiser, *Minister Rejects Bank's Appeal.* (January 9, 1964)

Calm and consolidation

Pauline Hodder, *'Rubbish' Of Course You Can Draw.* (Unpublished MSS)

Wendy Wilson, *Off Her Trolley.* Prep School, IAPS, (Summer, 1991)

Shirley Massey, *Music at Maltman's Green, 1975–1996.* (Unpublished MSS, 2003)

CHAPTER 5   MRS ASPREY'S ERA

Shirley Massey, *Music at Maltman's Green, 1975–1996.* (Unpublished MSS, 2003)

Wendy Wilson, *Maltman's Green School Science Department 1974–2000.* (Unpublished MSS)

Pat Journet, *Notes on Physical Education.* (2003)

CHAPTER 6   MRS EVANS' ERA

Madeleine Evans, *Friends of Maltman's Green AGMs* – various speeches.

Madeleine Evans, *Notes.* (2003)

Shirley Massey, *Music Notes 1994–95.* Maltman's Green Magazine

Independent Schools Inspectorate, *All Round Education in ISC Schools, A Digest of Reports 2000-1.* (2002)

CHAPTER 7   MALTMAN'S GREEN TODAY

Julia Reynolds, *Notes. (2003)*

Independent Schools Inspectorate, *Inspection Report on Maltman's Green Preparatory School.* (March, 2000)

Maltman's Green Preparatory School Brochure. (2000)

Married names and titles of those who contributed or are quoted

Mary Behrens (Lady Flowers), Ruth Behrens (Mrs Pilkington),

Hazel Dodds (Mrs Paterson), Caty Early (Mrs Crawford), Eleanor Early (Mrs Beard),

Patsy Fowler (Mrs Kain), Christine Lever (Mrs Hutchinson),

Bubbles Lemon (Mrs Levi), Audrey Lovibond (Mrs Priestman),

Bridget Luard (Mrs Howell), Barbara McMurray (Mrs Thomas),

Dorothea McMurray (Mrs Williamson), Rosemary Naylor (Mrs Burdis),

Pamela Neal Green (Mrs Lee), Peggy Neal Green (Mrs Allso),

Jane Noel (Mrs Skelton), Alison Nugent (Mrs Hirschberg), Mary Riley (Mrs Fox),

Helen Robinson (Mrs Anderson), Marian Robinson (Mrs Stamp),

Diana Sanderson (Mrs Hay), Susan Sanderson (Mrs Parkinson),

Olive Scott (Mrs Rutherford).

About the authors

Cynthia Walton lives in Solihull with her husband. She is an old girl of Maltman's Green. She graduated from the London School of Economics – B.Sc. (Econ). She worked in documentary films and for the British Film Academy. After marriage, she moved to Birmingham and had four children. She worked as a research assistant at the Faculty of Commerce in Birmingham University and later worked for the Family Planning Association for many years. As a freelance journalist, she has published articles on consumer, social and health topics for *The Guardian* and *The New Statesman*. In 2001, she produced a book with Audrey Court about the family planning movement, *Birmingham Made a Difference 1926-1991*. In 2002, she published a book of poetry, *Three Voices, Three Visions*, written by three poets and illustrated by three artists.

Pauline E. Hodder lives in Chalfont St. Giles, Bucks. She graduated from the Royal College of Art – ARCA. On graduating, she worked in fabric design as the assistant Head Designer at Jacqmar. Later she went into the Print Design Studio at Marks and Spencer. She then became self-employed, working in textiles, graphic design and childrens' book illustration. She was, until retirement, a member of the Chartered Society of Designers. She had not intended to teach, but was asked to help out in the art department of Windsor High School, which led to a part-time teaching post there. In 1968, she came to Maltman's Green School as Head of Art and then stayed at the school for 21 years, teaching art and Italic handwriting.